Hospital Visitation Guide for Ministers

HOSPITAL VISITATION

GUIDE

FOR MINISTERS

BONNY V. BANKS

STEWARD PUBLISHING

Hospital Visitation Guide for Ministers
STEWARD PUBLISHING, Union, New Jersey

Unless otherwise noted, scripture quotations are from the Holy Bible, Authorized King James Version. Belgium: Thomas Nelson Publishers 2001. Used by permission.

Scripture quotations marked (NLT) are taken from the Holy Bible, New Living Translation, copyright © 1996, 2004, 2007 by Tyndale House Foundation. Used by permission of Tyndale House Publishers, Inc., Carol Stream, Illinois 60188. All rights reserved.

Requests for permission to use or reproduce material from this book should be directed to: Permissions@HospitalVisitations.com.

Banks, Bonny V.
    Hospital Visitation Guide for Ministers/ Bonny V. Banks
    Includes bibliographical references
    ISBN 978-0-9796106-4-6
    ISBN 0-9796106-4-8

Printed in the United States of America

The paper used in this publication meets the requirements of the American National Standard for Permanence of Paper for Publication and Documents in Libraries and Archives 239.48-1992.

Dedication

To my mother, a godly, compassionate
and discerningly skillful leader

Table of Contents

Dedication..*vii*

Acknowledgement...*xv*

Preface..*1*

Introduction...*3*

Scriptures for Healing...*7*

Part One

Preparation...*11*

Hospital Visits Begin At Home 13

A Sample Prayer of Preparation........................…...14

The Importance of Prayer 15

Anointing With Oil 19

Displays of Emotion 22

If You are Sick 23

Part Two

General Protocols 25

Patient Information 27

Clergy Identification........................... 27

Parking 28

Hospital Visiting Hours 29

Obtaining Visitors' Passes.................. 30

Observing Universal Precautions........... 32

Avoiding the Spread of Infection 33

Healthcare-Associated Infections (HAI) and

Methicillin-resistant Staphylococcus aureus

(MRSA) 36

Hand Washing Procedure..................... 40

Concerns About Infection 43

Personal Protective Equipment.............. 44

Patient Privacy.................................. 45

Concern About Treatment 46

Food and Flowers............................... 47

Part Three

The Visit *51*

A Word About Decorum 53

Before Entering a Patient's Room 59

When Hospital Personnel Are Present 61

Patients in Isolation 62

Entering a Patient's Room 64

Sharing Scripture With a Patient 67

Preparing to Pray for a Patient 68

Leading a Person to Christ (sample)................... 70

Sample Scriptures to Share With a Patient Upon

Ministering Salvation... 72

Baptizing a Patient... 76

Baptism Scriptures... 83

A Sample Prayer for Healing 85

Sharing Holy Communion With a Patient 86

Scriptures for Holy Communion 89

Patients Who Are Sleeping 91

Patients Who Are Sedated, Unconscious or
Comatose 92

Patients Who Are Dying 93

After Praying for a Patient 95

Upon Leaving a Patient's Room 96

Visiting Babies 97

Visiting the Elderly 98

Visiting the Mentally Ill 99

Visiting the Chronically Ill 101

Part Four

Practical Insights *103*

Health and Life Insurance 105

Advance Directives: Living Wills, Durable Power of
Attorney for Healthcare, Healthcare Proxy and
Do Not Resuscitate (DNR) 109

Quality of Life 114

Choosing an Advance Directive 116

Two by Two 120

Part Five

Counsel and Comfort *123*

Helping Patients and Families Make

Tough Decisions 125

When Death Seems Imminent 129

Organ and Tissue Donation 133

Understanding Hospice Care 138

What to Do if a Patient Dies 143

Aftercare for the Family 144

Conclusion...................................*149*

Pleasing the Audience of One..............151

Thank you 161

Resources 163

Index...................................169

Acknowledgement

Special thanks to you, Father, for Your
guiding love and enduring grace.
Thanks to my family for your
invaluable support and encouragement.
Thank you to all who visit and
pray for the sick.

Preface

"For I was an hungered, and ye gave me
meat: I was thirsty, and ye gave me drink: I was a
stranger, and ye took me in: Naked, and ye
clothed me: I was sick, and ye visited me: I was in
prison, and ye came unto me [...] In as much as
ye have done it unto one of the least of these my
brethren, ye have done it unto me."

Jesus Christ

It is possible, albeit quite plausible to
consider that there is something special to God
about caring for those who are suffering. In all
of our spiritual endeavors and pressing toward
the mark, as mentioned by the great Apostle
Paul, we realize that reaching the high calling of
which the apostle speaks ultimately requires the
losing of our lives for Christ's sake – that is the
dedication of our time, prayers and resources

to be instruments of grace for the betterment of others. As God's workmanship, created in Christ Jesus and thoroughly furnished unto good works, we walk holding dear the requirements of faithfulness and love, which we demonstrate by keeping the great commandments. We are indeed our brother's keeper. *"Pure religion and undefiled before God and the Father is this, to visit the fatherless and widows in their affliction, and to keep himself unspotted from the world"* (James 1:27).

Jesus, the first born of many brethren and our ultimate example, visited the sick and the dead. Moved with compassion, Jesus interrupted, or so it would appear, many of his journeys to minister to the infirmed in body and soul. Often Jesus approached those who could not see Him and those who dared not even petition Jesus' grace. Bowed down, broken and weary, some had all but given up the fight. Today, Jesus calls out to the suffering and broken, through us, to be loosed from their infirmities.

Introduction

"By the sick, I do not mean only those that keep their bed, or that are sick in the strictest sense. Rather I would include all such as are in a state of affliction, whether of mind or body; and that whether they are good or bad, whether they fear God or not."

John Wesley

When visiting the sick you will encounter believers and non-believers alike. You will encounter lovers of Jesus and haters of God. You will meet Christians who are joyful and Christians who are disappointed, disillusioned, depressed and full of despair. You will stand at bedsides and look into sullen eyes that question God's faithfulness. Peace filled believers will encourage you as they march toward death's door.

Imagine having to witness suffering beyond the ability of any human to comprehend. You will long to caress children, whose frail bodies curved with disease, shame complaining hearts. Eyes will fasten upon you as saints and sinners search for answers. Are you up to the task? If you answered, "Certainly not," you are right and perhaps ripe for the undertaking.

As in antiquity, contemporary gates of Bethesda encircle many who are resigned, reconciled and resolute to live with illness and disease while hope fades by the day, month, year and decade. John Wesley aptly reminds us that affliction knows no boundaries of beliefs, proximity, status or character. It is our assignment, therefore, to look beyond the outward appearance, to behold the image and likeness of God, to remember how precious each of God's creatures is to Him.

Jesus is the healer, the burden bearer, the deliverer of grace unfathomable and the supreme author of peace. We are merely His messengers. We go as ambassadors representing the King of all Kings to extend Jesus' arms in love to those for whom Jesus shed His precious blood. We refrain from judging and condemning. The Apostle Paul asks, *"Who is he that condemneth? It is Christ that died, yea rather, that is risen again, who is even at the right hand of God, who also maketh intercession for us" (Romans 8:34).*

Remember, God sent not His Son into this world to condemn the world, but that the world through Him might be saved (John 3:17). Let us, as students of the Holy Spirit, eagerly set aside our inclinations and subdue our notions and emotions. Let us discipline our discernments to rather discover the limitless power of God's love and mercy toward His creation.

Let us, therefore, walk in the Love of God and leave the proving to God alone. Let us walk in the expectancy of God's mercy and grace that heal. Let us walk in wisdom and meekness, considering our own selves lest we fall, lest we offend. Let love prevail. Love never fails. Love melts hearts and soothes fears. Love assures and reassures. Love is kind. Love empathizes and sympathizes. Love accepts. Love speaks and love keeps silent. Love prays so that all present can understand. Love defers to wisdom. Love defers to itself.

Scriptures for Healing

"Surely he hath borne our griefs, and carried our sorrows: yet we did esteem him stricken, smitten of God, and afflicted. But he was wounded for our transgressions; he was bruised for our iniquities: the chastisement of our peace was upon him; and with his stripes we are healed."

Isaiah 53:4-5

"Bless the LORD, O my soul, and forget not all his benefits: Who forgiveth all thine iniquities; who healeth all thy diseases;"

Psalm 103:2-3

"Who his own self bare our sins in his own body on the tree that we, being dead to sins, should live unto righteousness: by whose stripes ye were healed."

I Peter 2:24

"The Spirit of the Lord is upon me, because he hath anointed me to preach the gospel to the poor; he hath sent me to heal the brokenhearted, to preach deliverance to the captives, and recovering of sight to the blind, to set at liberty them that are bruised."

Luke 4:18

"The centurion answered and said, Lord, I am not worthy that thou shouldest come under my roof: but speak the word only, and my servant shall be healed."

Matthew 8:8

"And Jesus said unto the centurion, Go thy way; and as thou hast believed, so be it done unto thee. And his servant was healed in the selfsame hour."

Matthew 8:13

"Jesus Christ the same yesterday, and today and for ever."

Hebrews 13:8

"And Jesus went about all the cities and villages, teaching in their synagogues, and preaching the gospel of the kingdom, and healing every sickness and every disease among the people."

Matthew 9:35

"Heal me, oh Lord, and I shall be healed; save me, and I shall be saved: for thou art my praise."

Jeremiah 17:14

"O LORD my God, I cried unto thee, and thou hast healed me."

Psalm 30:2

"He sent his word, and healed them, and delivered them from their destructions."

Psalm 107:20

"For I will restore health unto thee, and I will heal thee of thy wounds, saith the Lord;"

Jeremiah 30:17a

"Is any sick among you? let him call for the elders of the church; and let them pray over him, anointing him with oil in the name of the Lord. And the prayer of faith shall save the sick, and the Lord shall raise him up; and if he have committed sins, they shall be forgiven him."

James 5:14-15

"Confess your faults one to another, and pray one for another, that ye may be healed. The effectual fervent prayer of a righteous man availeth much."

James 5:16

"Beloved, I wish above all things that thou mayest prosper and be in health, even as thy soul prospereth."

III John 1:2

"And this is the confidence that we have in him, that, if we ask any thing according to his will, he heareth us: And if we know that he hear us, whatsoever we ask, we know that we have the petitions that we desired of him."

I John 5:14-15

Part One

Preparation

"And I sought for a man among them that should make up the hedge, and stand in the gap before me..."

Ezekiel 22:30

"Love is intercession on its knees..."

Karen Walden

11

Hospital Visits Begin At Home

Hospital visits begin with your private prayers for the sick. As you spend time in prayer, earnestly intercede for those who are suffering from illness. According to Isaiah 53:5 and 1 Peter 2:24, healing is God's will. The scriptures in 1 John 5:14-15 and Isaiah 55:11 assure us of the integrity of God's promise to keep His word. Seek the Lord for His Spirit of grace and anointing as you prepare to visit the sick.

By God's grace, God may use you to minister healing to many. Always remember Psalm 115:1, *"Not unto us, O LORD, not unto us, but unto thy name give glory, for thy mercy, and for thy truth's sake."*

Visiting patients in the hospital is a divine privilege that God has allowed you to have. When visiting patients, keep in mind the following procedures for etiquette, respect, protocol and safety. In 1 Corinthians 14:40 the Apostle Paul teaches that God is the author of order. *"Let all things be done decently and in order."*

A Sample Prayer of Preparation

Father, in the name of Your precious Son and my Savior, Jesus Christ, I thank You for the privilege You have given me to visit and pray for the sick. I thank You that in all diagnoses and prognoses Your healing power prevails. I thank You, Father, that You gave Jesus a name that is above every name and that all sickness, illness, infirmity, and disease bow before the power of Jesus' great name. I thank You, Lord Jesus, that Your sacrifice condemned sin in the flesh and made all provision for life and healing. By Your stripes all were healed. It is in You, Father, that I live and move and have my being. I thank You for Your grace that enables me to walk in faith on behalf of Your people. Thank You for healing every one today, Father. Bless me to be an instrument of Your grace and to proclaim with my life that all glory belongs to You; In Jesus' name, Amen.

The Importance of Prayer

Before beginning and at the conclusion of a hospital visit, always pray for God's covering and protection. As you begin your visit, pray as well for God's anointing to provide His guidance in your choice of words. The Lord will prepare your heart as you seek to be an instrument of His grace and love toward those you visit.

It is important to pray at the conclusion of the visit to refresh your spirit and remove any feelings of oppression or heaviness before returning to your home or office. Understand that sickness and disease are often mere physical occurrences. However, there are times when oppression or other spiritual malady is plaguing an individual. For this reason, be careful to pray earnestly for God's covering when you visit. As well, listen for the Holy Spirit's guidance in choosing your visits. If you are unexplainably hesitant or fearful about conducting a particular visit, refrain from going until or unless you are confident of the Holy Spirit's leading.

A lifestyle of prayer and fasting is often required for what may be *hard cases*. Because spiritual oppression can sometimes manifest in physical sickness, confronting certain infirmities requires faith developed from consecration and a thorough understanding of grace. Consider the early experience of Jesus' disciples as recorded in Matthew 17:14-21.

And when they were come to the multitude, there came to him a certain man, kneeling down to him, and saying, Lord, have mercy on my son: for he is lunatick, and sore vexed: for ofttimes he falleth into the fire, and oft into the water. And I brought him to thy disciples, and they could not cure him. Then Jesus answered and said, O faithless and perverse generation, how long shall I be with you? how long shall I suffer you? Bring him hither to me. And Jesus rebuked the devil; and he departed out of him: and the child was cured from that very hour. Then came the disciples to Jesus apart, and said, Why could not we cast him out? And Jesus said unto them, Because of your unbelief: for verily I say unto you, If ye have faith as a grain of mustard seed, ye shall say unto this mountain, Remove hence to yonder place; and it shall remove; and nothing shall be impossible unto you. Howbeit this kind goeth not out but by prayer and fasting.

Mustard seed faith is faith that develops, matures and evolves over time, through both experience and the appreciation of grace.

Jesus' objective in healing the sick was to demonstrate the power of love, mercy and grace to overcome the failings, weaknesses or oppressions of humankind. *"News about him (Jesus) spread far beyond the borders of Galilee so that the sick were soon coming to be healed from as far away as Syria. And whatever their illness and pain, or if they were possessed by demons, or were epileptics, or were paralyzed he healed them all" (Matthew 4:24 NLT).*[1]

Jesus healed compassionately and without condemnation, even when the cause of sickness

---

[1] *Holy Bible, New Living Translation.* Wheaton: Tyndale House Publishers, Inc.1996.

was unflattering to the individual. *"And, behold, they brought to him (Jesus) a man sick of the palsy, lying on a bed: and Jesus seeing their faith said unto the sick of the palsy; Son, be of good cheer ; thy sins be forgiven thee" (Matthew 9:2).*

In the case of a blind man from John 9:1-3, Jesus shared with His disciples (who inquired about the cause of the man being born blind) that the man's blindness was only to demonstrate the glory of God.

And as Jesus passed by, he saw a man which was blind from his birth. And his disciples asked him, saying, Master, who did sin, this man, or his parents, that he was born blind? Jesus answered, Neither hath this man sinned, nor his parents: but that the works of God should be made manifest in him.

The Holy Spirit may choose to reveal spiritual sickness to you. Be cautioned, however, to refrain from judging or announcing your perceptions to the patient or other individuals. Trust in the Holy Spirit's desire and ability to minister to the intimate chambers of a patient's heart as only the Holy Spirit can. Remember that the Holy Spirit's purpose in revealing precious secrets to you is to guide you in wisdom and intercession. Treat the Holy Spirit's trust with honor and fidelity.

Anointing With Oil

Typically, patients are appreciative of your prayers and visit alone.

When visiting those of like faith, you may perceive that the patient would like to be anointed with oil. Anointing with oil should be done at the request or consent of the patient or the patient's family. If you ask, be sure to pose the question as a preference to the patient rather than your seeking permission. Ailing patients will often grant an imposing request out of appreciation for the visit, a desire to please or a wish to avoid offending you. Many patients welcome the anointing with oil. However, patients who are unfamiliar with the practice of anointing with oil may find the suggestion imposing or unsettling. For those who have yet to either understand or prefer the anointing of oil, God's healing still prevails. Remember, it is the prayer of faith that shall save the sick (James 5:15).

Anointing with oil should be done discretely and without causing pain or discomfort to the patient. It is important that you have your anointing oil ready and prepared. Prior to your visit, you can purchase a jar of olive oil and, after praying over it and consecrating it for anointing, pour a small amount into a tiny vial. Tightly cover the container and carry it with you to the visit.

When preparing to anoint a patient with oil, carefully notice the posture and position of the patient. Often, a patient who is familiar with the anointing of oil will expect you to anoint her forehead. However, always ask permission to touch a patient.

If the patient's forehead is uncovered, ask the patient *if* you may anoint her forehead. If the patient's forehead is covered with bandages, for example, you may ask if the patient would prefer that you anoint her hand. If so, notice the hand that is free from intravenous needles, surgical wounds or bandages of any kind. Be careful to avoid touching any place that is encumbered or painful to the patient. If the patient's forehead or hands are unavailable for anointing, you may ask the patient where she would prefer to be anointed. You may also gently anoint over a sheet or blanket. It is unnecessary for you to touch the patient's bare skin.

Have your anointing oil ready and prepare to pray. Place a dab of oil on your forefinger noticing the patient at all times. You may choose to anoint in the shape of a cross or with a single dab of oil, depending on the condition of the patient. As you anoint the patient, call the patient's name and say, "I anoint you in the name of Jesus Christ. Be healed in Jesus' name." You may continue a brief prayer of healing while removing your hand from the patient.

Displays of Emotion

Hospitalized patients are in need of your faith, support and encouragement at all times. Sudden sickness, serious or prolonged illness, accidents and unexpected life changes can produce the effects of fearfulness and anxiety in patients. While it is natural for you to feel empathy and compassion for those who are suffering, note that patients can sense fear, nervousness and alarm from those who visit. What patients really want and need from you is calm assurance. Patients want to believe that God's love abounds and that God's presence, healing power and will to heal prevail over all diagnoses.

It is essential to maintain your faith and composure at all times. Keep from staring or tearing in a patient's presence. Patients will look to you as source of confidence and strength, even in the direst of conditions with the gravest of prognoses.

If You are Sick

When patients are in the hospital and suffering from illness, their immune systems, in many cases, have become compromised and are weaker. If you are suffering from a contagious illness, such as a cold or flu, please refrain from visiting patients until you are completely well. In this way, you will avoid exposing patients to harmful germs that could aggravate their current conditions.

As well, it is important for you to protect your immune system from further compromise. When you are ill, your body needs strength to fight against imposing infections. Many public institutions, including healthcare facilities, are replete with air borne contagions that only need be inhaled to cause or aggravate an illness. Be careful to protect yourself as well as patients by visiting when you are well.

While it may be a noble jester to deny your need for rest and recuperation in order to make the sacrifice to visit the sick, keep in mind that those you are visiting are vulnerable as well. When you exercise care to protect patients from germs, you honor your commitment to God for patients' healing and well-being.

Part Two

General Protocols

"*Wisdom is the principal thing; therefore get wisdom: and with all thy getting get understanding.*"

King Solomon

Patient Information

Before visiting the hospital facility, call patient information to confirm that the person you are planning to visit is there and receiving visitors. As conditions vary and protocols are underway, patients are often moved or undergoing tests or procedures at various times during their hospital stay. Calling ahead can help to ensure that you visit at an opportune time.

Clergy Identification

Be sure to carry your clergy identification to the hospital with you. Clergy identification distinguishes you as one visiting in an official capacity to pray and offer spiritual comfort.

Parking

Always park in designated public parking areas and obey all hospital parking regulations, including leaving fire lanes free for emergency vehicles and patients being discharged.

Many hospitals assess fees for parking. However, with clergy identification, security may allow you to park without a fee. Upon entering a hospital facility, check with security to have your parking ticket validated. Have your clergy identification ready to present. Without it, hospital security may decline to validate your parking ticket and you may have to pay for parking.

Note that in some facilities, such as state hospitals, a procedure to validate parking for clergy may be unavailable. It is a good idea to check with security before parking in a fee based area.

Hospital Visiting Hours

Hospital policies include specific hours of visitation in order to maximize time for patient rest and recuperation. Visits, although welcomed, can be tiresome to patients and for this reason, hospital personnel designate certain hours for visitation. It is a way of ensuring that patients benefit from specific uninterrupted periods of rest. As a minister, it is your duty to demonstrate respect for all hospital regulations and the patients you visit. Many hospitals allow regular visits from about 11:30 AM until 8:00 PM daily.

Note that the visiting hours for maternity, pediatric, critical care, intensive care and psychiatric units may vary. If you are visiting someone in a specialized unit of the hospital, obtain information on visiting hours before venturing to the facility.

The only time that you, as a minister, should attempt a visit in any unit outside of the regulated times is if there has been a severe emergency and you are specifically called by the patient, the patient's family member or a member of the patient's medical team to respond to the hospital right away.

Obtaining Visitors' Passes

After entering the hospital, go to the patient information desk. Wait your turn and ask for a visitor's pass to see the particular patient you are there to visit. You may be asked the purpose of your visit. If asked, respond by saying that you are clergy there to visit briefly with the patient. You may then be asked to display your clergy identification and directed to sign in a clergy roster, which is usually located at the patient information desk or held by security. In almost all cases, you will be able to obtain a visitor's pass.

On occasion, desk personnel may inform you that the patient currently has the maximum allowable visitors and that you have to wait until someone else who is visiting the patient returns. If you know the patient is expecting you, you may call the patient's room and, without requesting someone to leave, let the patient know that you are there. The patient may indicate that another visitor is leaving and ask you to come to the room. If not, you may decide to wait or return at another time.

It is important to understand that security and information desk personnel have discretionary rights that permit them to disallow visits by anyone whom they believe is compromising patient safety or disobeying hospital regulations.

Observing Universal Precautions

Universal Precautions are practical infection control measures developed by the United States Centers for Disease Control (CDC) to restrict the risk of transmission of blood borne pathogens spread by specific body fluids and blood. More specifically, hospital safety procedures that are in keeping with CDC recommendations are designed to protect patients, hospital personnel, and visitors from infections caused by the spreading of germs. Be careful to take Universal Precautions seriously as you will protect yourself and help to curtail the spread of infectious diseases to patients. Utilize the following Universal Precautions for visiting all patients at all times.

1. Wash your hands before entering any patient's room in order to ensure that you are not bringing germs into a patient's environment.

2. When in a patient's room, refrain from handling patient articles, tables, phones etc. unless requested.

3. When approaching a patient, refrain from freely touching the patient unless the patient indicates that she wishes to be touched.

4. Wash your hands after leaving a patient's room and before entering another patient's room.

Avoiding the Spread of Infection

There are many harmful germs consisting of bacteria, viruses, fungi and parasites.[1] Bacteria and viruses may be among the most easily

---

[1] US National Library of Medicine, National Institutes of Health "Infectious Diseases." Bethesda, Maryland, 2005.

spread in hospital settings, although fungi and parasites remain of serious concern.

Bacteria are one-celled organisms that mostly serve to facilitate health and healing in the body by destroying harmful cells and aiding in digestion. However, there are harmful bacteria that release toxins into the body to spread infection. For example, the bacteria, streptococcus and staphylococcus cause infections including strep throat, pneumonia, toxic shock syndrome, and certain kinds of skin and blood infections.

Viruses are capsules that invade the body to cause colds and influenza. If you have strep throat or a cold, for example, or have had recent contact with someone who has, avoid visiting the sick until you are certain that you are completely well and uninfected.

Fungi are germs that can get onto the skin by lingering on surfaces. Fungi can also be inhaled as air bone spores causing infection in the lungs. Fungi, while harmful in some cases, are mostly undisruptive. Be careful to note, however, that a weakened immune system can be vulnerable to fungi that are air borne or on surfaces.

Parasites are germs that attempt to live in or on the body and in food. Infections spread by parasites usually begin with contaminated food or water.

When visiting patients, be careful to observe Universal Precautions, as you will protect those you visit as well as yourself and your family. Understanding germs and how to avoid the spread of contagions will help you to make informed decisions about cleanliness – specifically, hand hygiene.

Healthcare-Associated Infections (HAI) and Methicillin-resistant Staphylococcus aureus (MRSA)

Healthcare-associated infections are caused by the introduction of harmful bacteria, viruses and fungi into a patient's bloodstream or onto a patient's skin while a patient is in a hospital or other healthcare facility. Healthcare-associated infections are so named because of their origin. When a patient becomes infected in the hospital and as a result of a hospital stay, the infection is considered healthcare-associated. According to the CDC, two million people annually - that is 1 in every 20 patients acquire a hospital-associated infection and for nearly 90,000 patients, the infections prove fatal. [2]

Methicillin-resistant Staphylococcus aureus (MRSA) is one type of hospital-associated infection. MRSA is a staph bacterium that can

---

[2] "Hhs Action Plan to Prevent Healthcare-Associated Infections." Washington, DC: Department of Health and Human Services, 2009.

get into the bloodstream through surgical sites, particular organs or onto the skin. Of particular concern for patients and healthcare workers is that the most life threatening MRSA infections tend to occur in hospitals and other healthcare facilities.[3] The main challenge with MRSA is its resistance to most known antibiotics. Therefore, the best approach to MRSA to date is prevention.

MRSA is a contagion and can be especially dangerous for individuals with compromised immune systems. MRSA has been known to cause surgical site infections, skin and blood infections, as well as infections in the urinary tract and lungs. Many healthcare facilities test for the presence of MRSA upon patient admission in order to ascertain the origin should a MRSA infection occur during hospitalization.

There are explanations for the cause and spread of hospital-associated infections, including MRSA. According to the CDC, the

---

[3] Ibid

major causes of the spread of MRSA include improper hand hygiene among healthcare personnel and improperly used or unsanitary medical equipment.[4] Frequently, MRSA affects the skin and can be spread through touch. One can spread MRSA by touching an infected individual or object that has the MRSA bacterium on it and then touching another person. The MRSA bacterium has been detected on patient personal items, including shavers, towels, bandages and other items that come in close contact with the skin. MRSA has also been detected on patient curtains in hospital rooms.[5]

When visiting patients, avoid handling patients' belongings or touching patients without permission. You may be avoiding the spread of a potentially lethal contagion. One major initiative for the prevention of hospital-associated infections like MRSA, aside

[4] "Causes of MRSA Infections: How MRSA Is Spread in the Community." Atlanta, Georgia: Centers for Disease Control and. Prevention, 2010.

[5] Michael Ohl, MD. "Hospital Privacy Curtains Are Frequently and Rapidly Contaminated with Potentially Pathogenic Bacteria." In *51st Inter Science Conference on Antimicrobial Agents and Chemotherapy*. Chicago, Illinois, 2011.

from educating medical personnel, patients, families, and the public, is the legal requirement for frequent and conscientious hand washing. [6]

Note: If you are pregnant or nursing, avoid visits where you know the patient has been exposed to MRSA or any other contagion. While the exposure to MRSA by an expectant mother may cause few problems, if any, for the unborn child initially, it is advisable to avoid contact with anyone who has a MRSA infection until you are no longer pregnant or nursing. There is a risk that an expectant mother infected with MRSA can pass it on to the child during childbirth. Additionally, particular antibiotics (Tetracyclines, for example) that can be used for the treatment of certain types of MRSA infections are ill-advised during pregnancy. [7]

---

[6] The American Recovery and Reinvestment Act of 2009, Public Law 111-5 (ARRA) is a federal law designed to provide for medical personnel training in the detection and prevention of Hospital-Associated Infections.

[7] Gorwitz, Rachel J., Jernigan, Daniel B., Jernigan, John A., Powers, John H. and Participants in the CDC Convened Experts' Meeting on Management of MRSA in the Community. "Strategies for Clinical Management of MRSA in the Community: Summary of an Experts' Meeting Convened by the Centers for Disease Control and Prevention." Atlanta, Georgia, 2006.

Hand Washing Procedure

Hand washing is an essential requirement for visiting patients. There are restrooms and hand washing stations available for this purpose. Please observe the following procedure for washing your hands.

1. Retrieve a clean paper towel

2. Use the paper towel to turn on the water at the sink

3. Wet your hands with warm water

4. Leave the water running

5. Use the paper towel to dispense a generous amount of soap onto your hands

6. Lather your hands

7. Rub hands together thoroughly. Be sure to cleanse the palms of your hands, the backs of your hands, and the front and back of your fingers, between your fingers, your thumbs and under your nails.

8. Clean your hands and wrists for 15-30 seconds

9. Rinse your hands and wrists

10. Retrieve a fresh paper towel

11. Dry your hands and wrists

12. Use the paper towel to turn off the water

13. If in a restroom, use the paper towel to handle the door knob and open the door

14. Discard the paper towel

Hand washing should be completed before and after visiting each patient. During certain visits, you may be requested to wear protective equipment like gloves. **Be cautioned, however, that putting on gloves without hand washing is ineffective against the spread of harmful contagions.** [8] Touching gloves with unclean hands contaminates the gloves.

Many hospitals and other healthcare facilities have hand sanitizer stations positioned near elevators, along the walls and in patient rooms. While the use of hand sanitizer is convenient, most only reduce the number of germs on hands and are unable to rid the hands of some types of germs. [9] Additionally, hand sanitizer is ineffective when hands are visibly dirty. [10]

Proper hand washing with soap and water provides the most thorough cleanse by

---

[8] "Hand Hygiene in Healthcare Settings." Atlanta, Georgia: Center for Disease Control and Prevention, 2011.

[9] "Handwashing: Clean Hands Save Lives." Atlanta, Georgia: Centers for Disease Control and Prevention 2011.

[10] Ibid

eliminating the most germs. If soap and water are unavailable, use at least a 60% alcohol-based hand sanitizer and rub hands together vigorously until dry.

Essentially, hand sanitizer provides less protection against germs than hand washing. The protection afforded by gloves requires that hands are clean before touching and placing on gloves.

Concerns About Infection

If you believe you have been exposed to MRSA or another pathogen as a result of conducting a hospital visit, refrain from attempting to self-treat and seek medical attention at once. Immediate detection and effective treatment present the best lines of defense against the worsening of a MRSA infection. MRSA, especially, is known to spread or become worse and even life threatening with delayed or improper treatment.

Personal Protective Equipment

Personal Protective Equipment consists of gear worn by health care workers and others, including visitors, to reduce exposure to communicable diseases. Personal Protective Equipment consists of gowns, gloves, masks, respirators, eye protection, and shoe coverings. Sample contagious diseases include, influenza (the flu), hepatitis A, hepatitis B, meningitis, pneumonia, strep throat, tuberculosis and, the common cold.

If in any way you are uncomfortable visiting a patient requiring that you wear personal protective equipment, please refrain from doing so.

Patient Privacy

Patient privacy is to be respected at all times. Patients' conditions and diagnoses are personal and are reserved for patients, patients' families and medical personnel only. When visiting patients, refrain from inquiring of patients, patients' family members or medical personnel about the nature of patients' illnesses, diagnoses, prognoses, or any other health-related information. This will ensure not only the preservation of patient dignity and privacy but also your adherence to the Health Insurance Portability and Accountability Act, also known as HIPAA.

HIPAA was originally enacted in 1996 to protect patient health care coverage with insurance companies. However, in April of 2003, legislators developed The Privacy Rule as a component of HIPAA. The Privacy Rule is designed to limit the inquiry and disclosure of patient Protected Health Information (PHI). PHI includes, but is not limited to, any information about a patient's health status, medical treatments and diagnosis.

Remember, as clergy, you are visiting in an official capacity, which is different from that of a family member, casual friend or acquaintance. With few exceptions, the protections afforded by HIPAA restrict medical personnel from discussing or sharing any portion of patient health information with anyone outside of the patient, unless otherwise indicated in writing by the patient.

In an emergency where a patient becomes incapacitated or incapable of making decisions, physicians may opt to contact a patient's immediate family to discuss life sustaining treatment options and recommendations.

Concern About Treatment

During a visit, a patient may share concerns with you relative to the treatment the patient is receiving at the hospital. On occasion, you may make an observation that arouses your concern as well. In either case, unless you are a member of the immediate family, refrain from addressing the issue directly or confronting hospital personnel. If you believe it is expedient to address a concern, share it with members of the patient's immediate family and defer to the family's judgment in handling the concern from there. If the patient is without family or close friends, you may share with the patient's healthcare advocate or healthcare proxy.

In almost all instances, there are facts and variables that weigh into the course of action (if any) the family prefers to take. Additionally, both the family and hospital personnel may be more informed than you are about the patient and the necessary manner of care required. **Exercise careful thought, caution and conviction in expressing your concerns.**

Food and Flowers

It is quite common for family members to take food items that are sure to bring smiles to patients. Traditionally, visitors have taken flowers to cheer ailing patients as well. In wondering whether to take food or flowers to patients, please consider the following.

Often, patients are observing strict diets that preclude the ingestion of certain items like salt and sugar, for example. In addition, there are times when patients are undergoing a series of tests that require fasting for hours or days at a time. When patients are undergoing tests or are in preparation for a surgical procedure, they are often classified "NPO" by their physicians.

NPO is from the Latin term, "Non Per Os," which means, "nothing by mouth." A patient classified, NPO, is restricted from ingesting food of any kind. Additionally, a NPO restriction means that a patient may neither have water nor ice chips for a specified time. Usually, at the doctor's discretion, a patient will end this fasting period with clear liquids in specific quantities.

Because diet is such a vital factor in healing and well-being, it is always best to defer to the regimen a patient's physician prescribes. Unless you are a member of a patient's immediate family who is certain of the patient's dietary allowances, it is best to refrain from taking food on your visit. Your good deed could otherwise impede the healing process.

Flowers add beautiful accents to any room and while usually appreciated, flowers may be inappropriate at times. First, many hospital protocols include the restriction of flowers in intensive care and critical care units. Secondly, some patients have allergies and other sensitivities that become aggravated by the fragrance and pollen in certain flowers. Lilies, for example, can be exquisitely pleasing to behold, yet too aromatic to stand, especially in a small or closed room.

Today, patients enjoy cards or uplifting reading materials. Friends, coworkers or family members often take balloons or other gift items they know their loved one would like to have close by.

In any case, the most important gift is your presence. Your smile and warmth are all you really need to carry. If you decide you want to take a gift, always consider the comfort and well-being of the patient you are visiting as well as that of any other patients who may be sharing that patient's room.

Part Three

The Visit

"I was sick, and ye visited me..."

Jesus Christ

A Word About Decorum

*"Let your conversation be as it becometh
the gospel of Christ..."*

Philippians 1:27a

Conversation is a manner of communicating. As a minister of the gospel, you communicate verbally through words in conversation, your comportment and the way you present yourself when visiting patients. Every form of self-expression carries an interpretative value for the patient and the patient's family.

Remember that conducting hospital visits is a divine privilege. Keep in mind the purpose of your visit, which is to bring healing and hope. Compassion and warmth are comforting to patients, but an unnerving experience can impede patient healing. Be careful to regularly check *your* emotional well-being and the subconscious assumptions that can arise unknowingly when encountering those facing adversity. Consider the following to avoid causing unintentional offense. The wise words of the Apostle Paul remind us, *"Let not then your good be evil spoken of" (Romans 14:16).*

Avoid taking casual observers with you to hospital visits. It is distressing for patients, who already feel vulnerable and exposed, to have inquisitive strangers staring down at them. Every person who enters a patient's hospital room should be there for a specific and significant purpose that directly benefits the patient. See that children and travel companions wait quietly for you in a designated area away from the patient's room. When you visit a patient without casual observers, you communicate respect for patient privacy and dignity.

Dress conservatively when conducting hospital visits. Let your adornment be that which is becoming of a minister at all times. Refrain from wearing apparel that could be considered overly casual, immodest or flashy. Avoid gaudy and distracting jewelry or accessories and noisy shoes. Your style of dress should demonstrate purposeful care in preparing to visit a patient in an official capacity as a minister. Remember that you are a representative of Christ. *"Let your moderation be known unto all men" (Philippians 4:5a).* When you demonstrate conscientiousness in your appearance, you communicate that the patient and the visit are important to you.

When conducting your visits, be sure to speak softly though with enough volume so that the patient you are visiting is able to hear and understand you without having to strain or ask you to repeat yourself. At the same time, refrain from speaking too loudly. Be careful to avoid comments or conversations that are best suited out of the presence of the patient. Keep in mind that ailing patients are usually able to hear very well, even if unable to communicate the same.

Address patients respectfully at all times. Refrain from using first names only unless invited or the patient is a child. Remain attentive and warm without becoming familiar. Keep a cheerful demeanor without gratuitous joking and gesturing. Avoid unsavory language, crude attempts at humor or trite assurances that can be interpreted as patronizing. Respectful speech communicates reverence to God and appreciation for the privilege of visiting and praying for His beloved.

Keep mobile and other electronic portable devices off or on silent when conducting hospital visits. Refrain from answering mobile phone calls or otherwise communicating electronically with others (including texting, reading or sending email) while in the presence of a patient or patient's family members. Avoid unnecessary interruptions in the visit. Dedicating your full attention to the patient and the patient's family during the visit communicates genuine interest and concern for the patient's well-being.

Refrain from eating or carrying your food or beverage with you to a patient's room. Avoid excessive gum chewing. Have your Bible, communion elements and vials for anointing or baptism easily accessible, if needed. When you are prepared and organized in your visit, the patient can better relax and trust you as an ambassador of Christ.

If a patient or patient's family members begin to confide in you or invite you to share, listen more than you speak and keep the focus of conversation on the patient. Refrain from questioning patients about their personal lives or illnesses. Refrain from giving unsolicited advice about any aspect of patients' personal lives or healthcare. Refrain from making or participating in disparaging commentary about anyone. Being quick to listen and slow to speak is both a virtue and an exercise in wisdom. *"Whoso keepeth his mouth and his tongue keepeth his soul from troubles" (Proverbs 21:23).*

Avoid dogmatic debates with patients or patients' family members. Refrain from making or participating in reproving commentary of any sort. Keep your opinions, especially about doctrinal matters, away from the center of conversation. Proving yourself right can be wrong for the patient. Remember your objective at all times. When visiting someone who is suffering, strive to be a cheerful blessing, an extension of Jesus' love. A patient should always feel better and encouraged as a result of your visit. The Apostle Paul shared great wisdom in his statement, *"All things are lawful for me, but all things are not expedient: all things are lawful for me, but all things edify not"* (*1 Corinthians 10:23*).

Avoid talking about yourself or your problems with patients. Your attempt to commiserate may be honorable. Yet, in so doing, you may lose the interest or attention of the patient. As well, in talking about your problems, you inadvertently burden the patient with the unneeded stress of comforting you.

Keep both your verbal and non-verbal communication free from any influences that could challenge your objective to be an instrument of peace, comfort, healing and the joy of the Lord. *"But as he which hath called you is holy, so be ye holy in all manner of conversation"* (*1 Peter 1:15*).

Before Entering a Patient's Room

Before entering a patient's room, always check that you have the correct name, room number and bed assignment. In many hospital facilities patient's names and bed assignments are displayed just outside the patient's door. Because there are times that you may not personally know the patient, this will ensure that you are entering the correct room and interacting with the exact person you are there to visit.

If you are unsure or the name display is indistinguishable, ask a nurse or aide at the nurse's station to confirm the room number and bed assignment of the patient you are there to visit. It is always advisable to make certain that you are at the correct room visiting the correct patient before entering.

Observe the outside of the patient's room to adhere to any postings that may be present. When medically necessary, hospital personnel may post signs requiring that Personal Protective Equipment be worn by everyone entering the patient's room. These postings are referred to as PPE's. Be careful to adhere to all such requirements before entering a patient's room. Most often, the purpose is to protect the patient from outside germs brought in by visitors.

As you approach the entryway to the patient's room gently knock on the door and wait for a response. When the patient answers, state your name and purpose for visiting, always addressing the patient by name. For example, "God Bless you, (Sister or Brother. . . Patient's name), I am Minister (Your name) from (Your church). I am here to pray with you." The patient may then invite you in.

When you initially knock and hear no response, it could be that the patient is attempting to dress or prepare before you enter. Wait for a moment and knock again before stepping into the room. If you walk into a room and notice the patient undressed or in the rest-room, step back out of the patient's room and assure the patient that you will wait outside until she is comfortably dressed or back in bed.

Usually, if not resting, the patient can let you know that she is aware of your presence. Assure the patient that you will wait outside until she is comfortably ready for you to enter.

Be willing to leave and return at another time if the present is inconvenient for the patient. Otherwise, wait for the patient to let you know when you may enter the room.

When Hospital Personnel Are Present

If there are hospital personnel present upon your arrival, they are either examining the patient or performing some other medically necessary function. Should hospital personnel enter the room during your visit, assure the patient that you can resume your visit after she receives the medical attention needed. Step back out of the room and wait completely outside and away from the door until hospital personnel have completed their care. You may observe nurses or doctors leaving the room. However, wait until they tell you that it is permissible to reenter.

Sometimes, hospital personnel leave a room temporarily just to retrieve a needed item and return right away. They know you are waiting and will usually tell you when you may reenter the room. Although patients may sometimes invite you to remain, always wait outside a patient's room while hospital personnel are present. Preserve and prioritize patient dignity by respecting patient privacy at all times.

Patients in Isolation

When patients are in isolation, it is because they may be suffering from contagious illnesses. Infections can be transmitted by airborne or other pathogens. As with all patients, when visiting a patient in isolation, be careful to observe the visiting regulations. You may be required to utilize Personal Protective Equipment. Remember, Personal Protective Equipment consists of gowns, gloves, masks, respirators, eye protection, and shoe coverings. If in any way you are uncomfortable visiting a patient in isolation, please refrain from doing so.

Patients in isolation are extra sensitive and can discern your discomfort. Your apprehension can cause increased anxiety for the patient and embarrassment for both of you. If you are unsettled, limit your visits to patient areas that are most comfortable for you. As you become seasoned, you may find your level of discomfort decreasing.

Note: If you are pregnant or nursing, consider refraining from conducting isolation visits.

Patients in Reverse Isolation

Patients in reverse isolation are in needed protection from harmful germs brought in by visitors. Exposure to outside germs threatens to compromise a patient's already weakened immune system. Therefore, visitors are required to wear Personal Protective Equipment.

The requirement to wear Personal Protective Equipment is more often to protect patients from germs brought in by visitors than the reverse. It is important to demonstrate complete compliance with visiting regulations at all times.

Entering a Patient's Room

When entering the room and approaching the patient, smile, greet any other patients that may be sharing the patient's room, restate your name and purpose for visiting. Acknowledge any other family members or persons who may also be visiting the patient. Observe the patient's posture, locations of other visitors, and medical equipment. Walk to the bedside that appears to be most comfortable for the patient. After walking to the patient's bedside, remain standing. Even if invited, refrain from sitting, especially on the patient's bed. Refrain from sampling any of the patient's food or handling patient possessions.

Be careful to look the patient in the eyes and smile lovingly at all times. When patients are in the hospital they may experience feelings of discomfiture, including loneliness, anxiety, fear, nervousness, and humiliation. Refrain from staring at the patient's body or machines. You could further embarrass or alienate the patient by your expressions. **Be conscientious of your countenance at all times.**

Extend love and greetings to the patient on behalf of the pastor and tell the patient her pastor is praying for her. For example, "Sister or Brother (Patient's name), pastor says to tell you that he (she) loves you and is praying for you and your family. How are you feeling today?"

After the patient says how she is feeling, ask if the patient needs anything. The patient may ask you to pour a cup of water or place an article close to her reach.

Note: When asking if a patient needs anything, be prepared to minister to a stated need without referring the patient elsewhere for help, even if it means going out of your way. You will avoid appearing disingenuous and the Lord will bless you for your sacrifice. *"And whatsoever ye do, do it heartily, as to the Lord, and not unto men; Knowing that of the Lord ye shall receive the reward of the inheritance: for ye serve the Lord Christ" (Colossians 3:23-24).*

Sharing Scripture With a Patient

Hearing God's word can give birth to and increase patients' faith. As you prepare to read a scripture, first ask if the patient would like you to. If so, ask the patient if she prefers that you read a particular portion of scripture. Many patients enjoy favorite passages from the Bible that bring comfort and assurance. Among them are Psalm 23, Psalm 91 and Isaiah 53:1-6.

When sharing a scripture, read the verses by putting in the patient's name where applicable. Maintain eye contact with the patient as much as possible. This helps the patient to personalize the scripture. Always choose uplifting passages that assure God's love through His words of faithfulness, peace, calm, healing and restoration. When you have finished reading the scripture, immediately prepare to pray.

If the patient does not want you to read a scripture, it could be that the person is tired, in pain or in such discomfort that she needs the visit to end quickly. Smile and immediately prepare to pray.

Preparing to Pray for a Patient

As you prepare to pray, observe the posture of the patient. If you believe the patient wants you to, ask the patient if it is okay to hold her hand and pray. Patients may sometimes reach for your hand. If so, gently hold the patient's hand (not the one with the intravenous needle in it because this can cause discomfort to the patient). Depending on a patient's posture, you may sometimes lightly rest your hand on top of a patient's hand as a gesture of affection or point of contact. Be mindful that sometimes it can cause pain to patients to be touched. There may be some patients who simply prefer not to be touched. If you are unsure, refrain from touching the patient.

Always allow the patient to remain as comfortable as possible. Reaching, turning or moving may be uncomfortable for patients. You may have to move to the other side of the patient's bed to accommodate the patient's existing position.

As you position yourself to pray, ask the person if she has received Jesus as Lord and Savior (or is saved). If the patient replies affirmatively, proceed with a brief prayer for healing. If the patient says that she is not saved, ask if the patient would like to receive Jesus into her heart.

Take a few minutes to share the gospel with anyone who is unfamiliar with the meaning of salvation. If the patient states that he or she would like to receive Jesus, begin the prayer by leading the person to Christ, then pray for healing and restoration.

If the patient is undecided or declines to receive Jesus, assure the patient of God's love for her and still pray for the patient's healing. Have a few salvation scriptures prepared to leave with the patient for leisure reading or further study at the patient's convenience. In this way, the word of God remains tangibly with the patient long after your visit has concluded. You are planting a seed that will yield increase as the patient experiences the love of Christ through you and others.

Leading a Person to Christ (sample)

Father, I believe that You so loved the world that You gave your only begotten Son, Jesus Christ, that whoever believes in Him should not perish but have everlasting life. I believe that Jesus died on the cross for my sins and was raised from the dead after three days. I repent for my sins and ask You, precious Jesus, to come into my heart and be my Lord, Savior, Healer, Redeemer and Friend, in Jesus' name, I pray. Amen."

Once you lead a person to Christ, visit often and remain in contact with the patient. It is important that you remain in close proximity to the patient to begin the discipleship process. Ask if the patient has or needs a Bible and, if needed, provide one. Point out significant scriptures from which the patient can begin to glean an understanding of God's grace, His plan for salvation, healing and a life of divine fellowship with Jesus. Ask if the patient has a home church. If needed, be prepared to recommend a Bible-based local church.

Sample Scriptures to Share
With a Patient
Upon Ministering Salvation

"For God so loved the world, that He gave His only begotten Son, that whosoever believeth in Him should not perish, but have everlasting life."

John 3:16

"In the beginning was the Word, and the Word was with God, and the Word was God. The same was in the beginning with God. All things were made by him; and without him was not anything made that was made. In him was life; and the life was the light of men."

John 1:1-4

"For by grace are ye saved through faith; and that not of yourselves: it is the gift of God: Not of works, lest any man should boast."

Ephesians 2:8-9

"And without controversy great is the mystery of godliness: God was manifest in the flesh, justified in the Spirit, seen of angels, preached unto the Gentiles, believed on in the world, received up into glory."

1 Timothy 3:16

"Therefore if any man be in Christ, he is a new creature: old things are passed away; behold all things are become new."

11 Corinthians 5:17

"But if we walk in the light, as he is in the light, we have fellowship one with another, and the blood of Jesus Christ his Son cleanseth us from all sin."

1 John 1:7

"My little children, these things write I unto you, that ye sin not. And if any man sin, we have an advocate with the Father, Jesus Christ the righteous: And he is the propitiation for our sins: and not for ours only, but also for the sins of the whole world."

1 John2:1-2

"Come now, and let us reason together, saith the LORD: though your sins be as scarlet, they shall be as white as snow; though they be red like crimson, they shall be as wool."

Isaiah 1:18

"There is therefore now no condemnation to them which are in Christ Jesus, who walk not after the flesh, but after the Spirit. For the law of the Spirit of life in Christ Jesus hath made me free from the law of sin and death."

Romans 8:1-2

"For whom he did foreknow, he also did predestinate to be conformed to the image of his Son, that he might be the firstborn among many brethren. Moreover whom he did predestinate, them he also called: and whom he called, them he also justified: and whom he justified, them he also glorified."

Romans 8:29-30

"For I am persuaded, that neither death, nor life, nor angels, nor principalities, nor powers, nor things present, nor things to come, Nor height, nor depth, nor any other creature, shall be able to separate us from the love of God, which is in Christ Jesus our Lord."

Romans 8:38-39

There are many, many scriptures from which you can choose to share with an individual upon ministering salvation. The gospel of John is a good starting point for a new Christian just beginning her walk with Christ.

Baptizing a Patient

There are times when a patient, upon receiving salvation, desires to be baptized. You may offer to baptize a newly saved patient or the patient may ask to be baptized. In either case, the subject of baptism should be treated reverently.

You will almost always be able to baptize a patient in a hospital or other healthcare facility. The manner in which you conduct the baptism depends upon the patient's condition, hospital policy and your physical ability and training. You may baptize a patient with or without full immersion in water. Remember that God's concern is for the condition of one's heart and is uninformed by a patient's physical limitations.

Baptizing a patient by sprinkling is the safest way to conduct baptism in a hospital setting. In the same way you would carry anointing oil, you may carry a vial of water you have already prayed over and consecrated for baptizing. You may also pray and consecrate water for baptism at a patient's bedside.

First, be sure the patient understands the significance and purpose of baptism. Baptism acknowledges the death, burial and resurrection of our Lord, Jesus Christ. When you baptize a patient, you lead the patient in a symbolic death of the former person through burial in a watery grave (submersion in water) and the patient's resurrection as a new creature. *"Therefore we are buried with him by baptism into death: that like as Christ was raised up from the dead by the glory of the Father, even so we also should walk in newness of life" (Romans 6:4).*

Avoid dogmatic discourse. Remember the wise words of the Apostle Paul, *"For as many of you as have been baptized into Christ have put on Christ" (Galatians 3:27).* Your appreciation and acceptance of God's insight into a person's heart should provide you the needed resolve to allow the Holy Spirit to lead in any discussion of the tenets of baptism.

Secondly, lead the patient in a brief prayer of repentance and acknowledgment of baptism unto Christ. It is unnecessary for the patient to expose or name individual sins aloud. It is to

God alone that the patient needs to open her heart completely. You would conduct the baptism by sprinkling similarly as you would by immersion. While the patient is sitting or lying comfortably, place a small amount of the consecrated water upon your finger tips and, depending on the condition and preference of the patient, you may allow a few drops of water upon the forehead or you may touch the forehead in one motion or in the shape of the cross. Proclaim the words of baptism.

If the patient is ambulatory and desires full immersion in water, proper protocol requires that you inquire of hospital personnel before baptizing a patient. The purpose for your inquiry is to ensure that you are abiding by healthcare facility procedures, which include allowing a patient's medical team to be informed and to make decisions pertaining to the patient's ability to be baptized by immersion.

It is ill-advised to attempt to conduct a baptism by immersion without informing hospital personnel and obtaining permission to do so. If granted permission by hospital personnel to baptize a patient by immersion, be sure to obtain information as to the time and place allowed. Inquire also about the availability of medical personnel to be present if needed. Liability is a major concern in healthcare settings and, as a minister, you accept responsibility for patient care and safety by operating within the boundaries established by the facility.

Additionally, in order to baptize anyone by full immersion in water, you should have both the physical ability and formal training in the technique. These imperatives help to ensure that you avoid injury to yourself or the patient.

Any time there is full immersion in water, a risk of drowning or other injury is of concern. Again, it is imperative that medical personnel be informed, present (for safety) and have given written permission for the baptism by immersion to take place. Written permission for baptism by immersion may be obtained by the patient or the patient's family.

In hospital or healthcare settings where the baptism is allowed, patients will usually have access to bathing or gym facilities. Commonly, patients choose a bathtub or if a Jacuzzi is available, patients may prefer it because of space. Be sure that the patient has proper attire for baptism. Baptism attire may include long shirts and slacks over swimwear or undergarments in order to ensure that the patient is fully covered during the baptism. Avoid baptizing in attire consisting only of swimwear or undergarments. As well, the patient should have a private changing area as well as a supply of dry clothing and hair drying equipment for after the baptism.

The following example is for illustration purposes only and should not be interpreted as step-by-step instructions for performing a baptism in a hospital or other setting. You should perform a baptism only if you have received formal training by your pastor or elder. Even if requested, refrain from attempting to perform baptisms by immersion in any setting, especially healthcare facilities, until or unless you have received formal training and/or certification and can demonstrate the same in writing.

Illustration: If you are baptizing a patient in a Jacuzzi, for example, you should be able to enter and stand alongside the patient. Allow the patient to sit in the water. Take note of the patient's height to ensure proper footing and the ability to immerse without hitting any portion of the bathtub or Jacuzzi. If you are baptizing a patient in a bathtub, you may be able to stand or kneel just outside the bathtub alongside the seated patient. Ensure that you are positioned in the most supportive fashion for both you and the patient.

Before beginning, explain each step the baptismal procedure will entail. When the patient tells you she is ready, steady your hands and proclaim the words of baptism as you would normally.

After speaking, gently immerse the patient in the water and immediately bring the patient back up. Be sure that the patient is breathing properly and can maneuver as before. The patient should be removed from the water immediately and provided a private space to change into dry clothes. Avoid celebration until the patient is completely out of the water, dressed in dry clothes and back in bed or seated comfortably in her room.

Remember, as a member of the clergy, you acknowledge the need to prioritize patient care at all times. Abiding by sacred principles of ministry, you operate in love, deferring to godly wisdom above all. Enthusiasm and zeal are commendable, but conscientiousness in your approach to patient care will prove invaluable. *"Wisdom is the principal thing; therefore get wisdom: and with all thy getting get understanding" (Proverbs 4:7).*

Baptism Scriptures

"Go ye therefore, and teach all nations, baptizing them in the name of the Father, and of the Son, and of the Holy Ghost:"

Matthew 28:19

"Then Peter said unto them, Repent, and be baptized every one of you in the name of Jesus Christ for the remission of sins, and ye shall receive the gift of the Holy Ghost."

Acts 2:38

"Then Philip opened his mouth, and began at the same scripture, and preached unto him Jesus. And as they went on their way, they came unto a certain water: and the eunuch said, See, here is water; what doth hinder me to be baptized? And Philip said, If thou believest with all thine heart, thou mayest. And he answered and said, I believe that Jesus Christ is the Son of God. And he commanded the chariot to stand still: and they went down both into the water, both Philip and the eunuch; and he baptized him."

Acts 8:35-38

"Therefore we are buried with him by baptism into death: that like as Christ was raised up from the dead by the glory of the Father, even so we also should walk in newness of life."

Romans 6:4

"Therefore if any man be in Christ, he is a new creature: old things are passed away; behold, all things are become new."

11 Corinthians 5:17

"For as many of you as have been baptized into Christ have put on Christ."

Galatians 3:27

"Buried with him in baptism, wherein also ye are risen with him through the faith of the operation of God, who hath raised him from the dead."

Colossians 2:12

A Sample Prayer for Healing

"Father, in the Name of Jesus, we acknowledge Your presence and thank You for Your love toward *Sister or Brother (Patient's name)*. Thank You, Father, that according to Your word in Isaiah 53:5, *'Sister or Brother (Patient's name)* is healed by Jesus' stripes and Jesus' blood makes *(Patient's name)* whole. We thank You that You sent Your word and healed *Sister or Brother (Patient's name)* and Your word cannot return unto You void. You send Your word out and it always produces fruit. Your word accomplishes all You want it to and it will prosper everywhere you send it. I pray that You grant *Sister or Brother (Patient's name)* Your grace to receive rest and complete restoration because she (or he) is Your beloved. Jehovah Rapha, You are the God that heals *Sister or Brother (Patient's name)* and we thank You for her (or his) healing in the name of Your Son, Jesus Christ, who is Lord and whose name is above every name. Amen." Always remember to pray God's word over patients. Remember, Isaiah 53:5 and 1 Peter 2:24.

If other family members or friends are present, ask God's blessings upon them as well.

Sharing Holy Communion
With a Patient

If the patient is a believer in the Lord, Jesus Christ, the patient may request communion or you may offer communion to a patient who you know or believe is a Christian.

In serving communion, observe that the patient is awake, alert and ready to receive communion. You may invite any visitors who are believers in the Lord, Jesus Christ to receive communion as well. Be careful to set up the communion items on a self-provided tray as to avoid impinging upon the patient's space at the bed table. If needed, you may substitute water for the juice and a tiny cracker for the bread. Assure the patient of God's love and appreciation for her desire for communion and the condition of her heart as mattering most to God.

Begin the communion ceremony by leading a prayer of repentance and forgiveness of others, acknowledging the significance of Jesus' sacrifice for sin. Consecrate and distribute the elements. Explain the purpose of Holy Communion so that everyone present understands. Read a communion scripture, such as 1 Corinthians 11:23-26.

For I have received of the Lord that which also I delivered unto you, That the Lord Jesus the same night in which he was betrayed took bread: And when he had given thanks, he brake it, and said, Take, eat: this is my body, which is broken for you: this do in remembrance of me. After the same manner also he took the cup, when he had supped, saying, This cup is the new testament in my blood: this do ye, as oft as ye drink it, in remembrance of me. For as often as ye eat this bread, and drink this cup, ye do shew the Lord's death till he come.

Assure the patient that she may take Communion daily in fellowship with the Lord. Many believers throughout the Body of Christ take Communion daily, especially for healing. Be careful to serve communion reverently and convey the same to the patient. The Apostle Paul admonishes against dishonor for the Lord's Supper. *"Wherefore whosoever shall eat this bread, and drink this cup of the Lord, unworthily, shall be guilty of the body and blood of the Lord" (I Corinthians 11:27).* If a patient is unclear about the meaning and significance of Holy Communion, pray with her instead and allow the Holy Spirit the time to minister. Perhaps upon a following visit the patient may be ready to commemorate Jesus' sacrifice with a clearer understanding.

Keep in mind that demonstrating regard for patient needs and hospital protocols is respectful to God and allows for the exercise of faith in the healing power of the Eucharist with a clear conscience and appreciation for Jesus' sacrifice.

Scriptures for Holy Communion

"And as they were eating, Jesus took bread, and blessed it, and brake it, and gave it to the disciples, and said, Take, eat; this is my body. And he took the cup, and gave thanks, and gave it to them, saying, Drink ye all of it; For this is my blood of the new testament, which is shed for many for the remission of sins."

Matthew 26:26-28

"And as they did eat, Jesus took bread, and blessed, and brake it, and gave to them, and said, Take, eat: this is my body. And he took the cup, and when he had given thanks, he gave it to them: and they all drank of it. And he said unto

them, This is my blood of the new testament, which is shed for many. Verily I say unto you, I will drink no more of the fruit of the vine, until that day that I drink it new in the kingdom of God."

Mark 14:22-25

"And he took bread, and gave thanks, and brake it, and gave unto them, saying, This is my body which is given for you: this do in remembrance of me. Likewise also the cup after supper, saying, This cup is the new testament in my blood, which is shed for you."

Luke 22:19-20

"But let a man examine himself, and so let him eat of that bread, and drink of that cup."

1 Corinthians 11:28

Patients Who Are Sleeping

If upon gently knocking on the door and you have yet to hear a response after some time, just above a whisper, greet the patient. State your name and purpose for visiting, "God Bless you, (Sister or Brother. . . Patient's name), this is Minister (Your name) from (Your church). I am here to pray with you." If you continue to wait for a response, the patient may be sleeping. Lean into the doorway and with as few light steps as possible, notice the patient.

If the patient is sleeping, it is because rest is an essential element of healing. In their efforts to recover from injury or illness, patients are sometimes taking medications that cause sleepiness. Refrain from approaching the patient's bed because you may wake the patient. Sudden surprises can cause unnecessary anxiety for patients and could make your visit less welcomed. Instead, gently back away, offer soft prayer at the entryway of the door and exit the room. Jesus hears you and though the patient may not be aware of your presence, Jesus is.

Patients Who Are Sedated, Unconscious or Comatose

When patients are sedated, unconscious or comatose, it could mean that the patient's infirmity or injury has caused significant damage to the body. At times, patient physicians treat patients with medications that serve to reduce pain.

As well, certain powerful medications are used to sedate patients. There may also be times when patients are unable to breathe on their own and are assisted by respirators or other artificial means. In these cases, you may quietly approach the patient's bedside.

Gently place your hand on top of the patient's hand and lean over to lightly whisper in the patient's ear. Tell the patient who you are and the purpose for your visit. Remember to extend love to the patient on behalf of your pastor.

If the patient is unsaved or if you are unsure of the patient's salvation, you may lead the person to Christ by whispering the prayer of salvation in the patient's ear. Proceed with the prayer of healing. Tell the patient that Jesus loves her, her pastor loves her and that you both will continue to pray for her.

If other family members or friends are present, ask God's blessings upon them. Ask if the patient needs anything. Extend love and continued prayers from your pastor and you. Gently back away and exit the room.

Patients Who Are Dying

Patients who are dying are often quiet and unresponsive. Some have ceased eating and talking. Family members are often present. Conduct the visit as you would normally.

Keep in mind that long after patients have stopped eating and speaking, they can still hear quite well. Anything discussed in the presence of a dying patient, however unresponsive, can likely be heard by the patient. Gently place your hand on top of the patient's hand lean over to lightly whisper in the patient's ear. Tell the patient who you are and your purpose for visiting. Remember to extend love to the patient on behalf of the pastor.

If the patient is unsaved or if you are unsure of the patient's salvation ask if you may pray a prayer of salvation for the patient. Look for any signs of agreement or decline. Honor the wishes of the patient at all times. If allowed by the patient or the patient's family, lead the patient to Christ by whispering the prayer of salvation in the patient's ear. Proceed with a prayer for healing. Tell the patient that Jesus loves her, her pastor loves her and that you both will continue to pray for her.

If other family members or friends are present, ask God's blessings upon them. Ask if there is anything the patient or family needs.

Extend love and continued prayers from your pastor and you. Gently back away and exit the room.

After Praying for a Patient

At the close of the prayer, assure the patient again that her pastor loves her and will continue to keep her in prayer, as will you. Gently back away from the bed and out of the room.

Although the patient may say that she is feeling well patients still need rest. It takes energy away from patients to receive visits, especially from clergy, because of the formality involved. Your visit should be completed in five to ten minutes.

Be careful, however, to avoid appearing rushed. A patient that wants or needs to talk may ask you to stay a bit longer, which is fine. Be mindful, however, that God's word, coupled with your presence and prayers are encouraging to patients and any strength a patient gains should be preserved as much as possible.

Upon Leaving
a Patient's Room

Upon leaving a patients room, go to the nearest rest-room or hand washing station (out of the view of the patient or the patient's family) and wash your hands. There are different types of germs present in hospital settings. It is important that you carry none home to your family.

Many patient rooms are equipped with sinks. However, at the conclusion of your visit, refrain from using the patient's sink or cleansing your hands where the patient can see you. Always use a rest room or hand washing station out of the sight of the patient or the patient's family. This allows you to wash your hands while preventing any misunderstanding or embarrassment to anyone.

Visiting Babies

When visiting babies be careful to exercise caution as babies are the most fragile of all human beings. A baby's parents should be present during the visit. As you enter the baby's room, identify yourself and purpose for visiting. Greet the parents, any other family members or friends that may be present and the baby, calling the baby by name. Express love to the parents and family on behalf of your pastor. Ask if there is anything the parents or baby needs.

As you position yourself to pray, approach the bedside of the baby. Refrain from picking the baby up or exciting the baby in any way. Refrain from leaning over the baby and breathing in the baby's face. As a sign of affection or point of contact, and with the parent's permission, gently touch the baby on the forearm with one finger (not on the baby's hands) as you begin to pray.

At the close of the prayer assure the parents again that the pastor and you love them and will continue to keep baby and the family in prayer. Gently back away from the bed and out of the room. Go to the nearest restroom or hand washing station (out of the view of the family) and wash your hands.

Visiting the Elderly

A good listener makes pleasant company for the elderly. Learn to follow their lead when visiting. Begin with your greeting and observe from there. If an elder wants to talk, listen. An elder may merely desire company to sit a while or play a game such as checkers. Always ask if there is anything you can do to for the patient and follow through. God will bless you.

Without promising, try to visit the elderly as a matter of routine. The elderly are often lonely and will look forward to your visit. If you miss your visit, the elder may still appreciate your call. For the elderly, consistency and quality matter more than the length of the visit. With every visit your presence declares, "You are not forgotten."

Visiting the Mentally Ill

Mental illness afflicts people of all ages, ethnicities, professions and religious affiliations. People suffering from mental illness are needful of the same empathy, compassion and careful consideration as those suffering physical illness. Because of the nature of mental illness and the stigma traditionally attached to it, patients who allow you to visit extend a valuable and special trust to you. Remember that as with all patients, Jesus entrusts you to refrain from judging.

When visiting the mentally ill, it is advisable to keep the visit brief without appearing hurried. Although appearing joyful at your arrival, keep in mind that a long visit can be distressing for the patient. As with patients who are physically ill, those who are mentally ill may become disquieted in an attempt to accommodate your presence for long periods. All patients need rest, including the mentally ill because exhaustion can occur on every level.

Keep in mind that mentally ill patients may also appear anxious at times and may petition your assistance in any number of areas including release from the hospital. You may even hear unfavorable allegations of mistreatment. Be sympathetic, yet try to avoid much discourse in any unconstructive vein. Focus the conversation on gratitude, God's love, faith and blessings. Your visit should leave the patient feeling strengthened and encouraged. Always endeavor to leave patients with a smile.

Share any patient's concerns with a member of the patient's family and allow the family to intervene on the patient's behalf. If the patient has no family members with whom to share what you believe to be a legitimate concern, share your concern with your pastor and defer to your pastor's instructions.

Visiting the Chronically Ill

Chronic illness is infirmity that is continual, persistent, stubborn, seemingly never ending, or reoccurring over long periods of time. Patients who suffer from chronic illness need consistency in care, prayer and encouragement. Try to visit on a regular basis, as the afflicting nature of chronic illness breeds loneliness and weariness in patients. Consistency and quality matter a great deal to the chronically ill. With every visit your presence declares, "You are not forgotten."

Part Four

Practical Insights

"*For the LORD giveth wisdom: out of his mouth cometh knowledge and understanding.*"

Proverbs 2:6

Health and Life Insurance

Undoubtedly, life and health insurance benefits inform treatment choices. Discussions surrounding insurance can sometimes take place at inopportune times, like when a patient needs coverage the most. Ideally, patients would do well to have the assurance of knowing that financial concerns can be avoided when in need of healthcare. As well, patients' family members can rest easy when insurance woes are absent in the midst of difficult times related to saying goodbye.

Often, patients who have neither health nor life insurance choose to forego the pursuit of needed medical attention. Patients should know that many public hospitals offer what is termed, *charity care*, for the uninsured. As well, certain federal and state governmental organizations that offer financial assistance for individuals, children and families also offer free or reduced price life and health insurance.

Additionally, United States Veterans qualify for health insurance that may include spouses and dependent children. Moreover, veterans qualify for burial benefits. For example, a veteran who expires in a hospital may qualify for burial benefits that include memorial services as well as interment. A veteran who expires at home may qualify for interment benefits. Depending on individual criteria, a veteran may qualify for life insurance as well.

As a minister, you may have the opportunity to encourage a patient or patient's family that has concerns about care as it pertains to health or life insurance. You can provide patients and families with educational material that may help in researching and obtaining adequate insurance to meet their individual and corporate needs. There are many resources available to share. Among the resources available are the following.

National Council on Aging: National Center for Benefits Outreach & Enrollment

1901 L Street, NW
4th Floor
Washington, D.C. 20036
202.479.1200
http://www.benefitscheckup.org/

Centers for Medicare & Medicaid Services

7500 Security Boulevard
Baltimore MD 21244-1850
1800-633-2273
http://www.medicare.gov

U.S. Department of Veterans Affairs

810 Vermont Avenue, NW
Washington, DC 20420
1-800-827-1000

Veterans Life Insurance:

Service members and/or Veterans Group Life Insurance Program 1-800-419-1473
All other VA Life Insurance Programs 1-800-669-8477
http://www.va.gov/

Advance Directives: Living Wills, Durable Power of Attorney for Healthcare, Healthcare Proxy and Do Not Resuscitate (DNR)

Contemporary hospital admitting procedures include inquiries about whether a patient has an Advance Directive. Increasingly, healthcare personnel are required to inquire and, in some cases, encourage patients to consider preparing an Advance Directive. In many instances medical personnel will suggest and even schedule a patient meeting with a facility social worker to discuss the uses and benefits of an Advance Directive.

Patients may become alarmed by the implications of Advance Directives. However, patients can be assured that inquiry about Advance Directives has become a matter of admission procedure irrespective of the purpose or length of the hospital stay. Hospital personnel are required to explain an Advance

Directive as a mechanism to allow patients to maintain power and control over their individual healthcare decisions.

Varying by state, there are different types of healthcare Advance Directives including: Living Will, Durable Power of Attorney for Healthcare, Healthcare Proxy, and Do Not Resuscitate. When inquiring about whether a patient has prepared an Advance Directive, some healthcare personnel may use the term, Living Will. Because a general Advance Directive and Living Will serve similar purposes and are sometimes interchangeable in various facilities, only one of the forms may be needed.

The main distinction between a general Advance Directive and a Living Will is that a general Advance Directive allows a patient to designate another party to make emergency healthcare decisions on the patient's behalf should the patient become incapacitated. Living Wills usually indicate the patient's express wishes in the case of incapacity without designating another individual with decision-making authority. Both a general

Advance Directive and Living Will consist of the patient's written instructions regarding the use of life saving procedures, including CPR, the use of ventilators and other mechanical equipment should the patient become consciously unable to make emergency decisions.

If a patient prefers to forego indicating written instructions in the case of incapacity, but prefers to entrust a loved one with the decision-making, the patient may prepare a Durable Power of Attorney for Healthcare or Healthcare Proxy, both of which allow for a designee to make healthcare decisions.

A Healthcare Proxy usually acts on behalf of a patient who, though alert and conversant, may be unable, through some disabling or hindering condition, to fully comprehend or process certain complexities related to her healthcare decision-making.

Note that the terms used to reference particular forms of Advance Directives can vary from state to state and are often used interchangeably. In some states, the distinguishing factors between the Healthcare Proxy and the Durable Power of Attorney are as follows: The designation of a Healthcare Proxy leaves all healthcare related decision-making up to the designated individual. The Healthcare Proxy is usually named on a one-page document without further detail. The Durable Power of Attorney assigns a designee, but also allows the patient to provide specific limitations as well as detailed instructions regarding aspects of her healthcare under particular conditions. A Durable Power of Attorney for Healthcare is more expansive, usually comprising several pages.

Another type of Advance Directive is a DNR. DNR is an acronym for "Do Not Resuscitate." A DNR order states that in the event a patient's heart and lung function appear to cease, cardiopulmonary resuscitation (CPR) should not be performed. Conventional CPR consists of timed chest compressions and mouth-to-mouth ventilation or for people preferring to avoid mouth-to-mouth ventilation, a rapid succession of chest compressions. In hospitals and many other public settings, resuscitation includes a process called defibrillation. Defibrillation is the use of electricity through paddles carefully placed on the outside chest cavity or heart itself to shock the heart back into a regular rhythm.

Patients who opt for a DNR order choose to forego CPR should a life-threatening emergency arise. The DNR order is signed by both the patient and the patient's physician and placed in the patient's chart. This document is referred to in the event that resuscitation would be needed to restore life to a patient who appears to have died.

Patients and families should know that a DNR can be modified or revoked at any time should the patient and family have a change of heart. If a change of heart occurs, the patient's physician and caretaker should be notified right away to have the patient's status updated. The DNR update includes the removal of the DNR order from the patient's chart.

All other Advance Directives can be modified or revoked as well. It is important to note that the patient or the patient's designated healthcare proxy has the authority to make changes to a patient's Advance Directive. A patient may also remove the designation of any previously authorized individual listed on a general Advance Directive. In some cases a patient may require legal assistance to dissolve a previously named Power of Attorney for Healthcare.

Quality of Life

Some patients and families consider quality of life discussions and opinions highly subjective, especially in the event of an emergency. For this reason, patients can utilize Advance Directives to define quality of life issues for themselves early in medical treatment or before treatment begins. A patient has the right to indicate on an Advance Directive the circumstances under which lifesaving treatments, including CPR, should be performed.

What one patient considers a quality life could easily be an unacceptable existence for another. For example, one patient may indicate a preference for CPR in every circumstance. Another patient may want CPR only in the event that her likelihood of functioning independently from a ventilator in the future can be at least presumed, if not assured by physicians. Another patient currently undergoing dialysis treatments may indicate a preference to continue the therapy only in the event that brain functionality remains unimpaired. Many patients equate quality of life with independence and self-sufficiency and choose to forego life-prolonging treatments likely to result in significant dependence upon machines or other people.

In defining quality of life individually, there are any number of specific instructions patients may give in preparing an Advance Directive. A patient can specify what life saving treatments the patient prefers at varying stages of health.

To specify her wishes, a patient may utilize an Advance Directive template provided by the healthcare facility as well as a self-written and signed communication to her physician or healthcare team outlining circumstances under which lifesaving treatments or therapies should be administered. As long as the self-prepared document can be authenticated, the patient can utilize it for advance instructions.

Choosing an Advance Directive

Many health care facilities have Advance Directive information and templates available for patients and their families to review, read, discuss and sign together. However, the review, discussion and decision-making process involved in preparing an Advance Directive should take time. Patients would do well to learn about Advance Directives before a hospital stay to ensure that the decision whether or how to prepare an Advance Directive is well thought out.

Advance Directives provide patients the benefit of knowing that their wishes are documented should the need arise for emergency decision-making. As well, patients' family members may be spared the painful and emotional difficulty of making life-altering decisions on behalf of their loved one, especially when unaware of the patient's wishes.

In the proper setting, patients, as well as patients' loved ones, tend to appreciate the discussions initiated by an inquiry about Advance Directives. Family members often find relief in knowing a patient's advance wishes, whether formalized in an Advance Directive or merely stated for the record.

While Advance Directives or Living Wills are voluntary, it is advisable for patients to discuss their wishes with their families or trusted loved ones. There are times, however, when patients may feel uncomfortable discussing their wishes with family members or other loved ones. In these cases, a patient may complete an Advance Directive to merely to inform family members of the patient's choices.

On rare occasions, a patient may entrust you as a minister to make emergency healthcare decisions on the patient's behalf. If a patient or patient's family asks for your input, it is important to remember that it is the desire of the patient that you must keep in mind. If you find that you may become involved in decision-making, consider it a sacred privilege. Pray without ceasing and keep the patient's family involved as much as possible except when requested by the patient to keep her request confidential. If a patient designates you to make emergency healthcare decisions should the patient become incapacitated, it should be so noted in the patient's chart.

When you know that a patient desires your input, for discussion, engage the patient in a conversation about her wishes. Sometimes, patients are more comfortable sharing wishes with loved ones or a minister than indicating their choices on a form. This may be due to a patient's discomfort with the inability to consider any unforeseen or extenuating circumstances affecting the volatility of a patient's health. As well, a patient needs to feel comfortable that any Advance Directive reflects the patient's most up-to-date preferences. Patients should know that Advance Directives or Living Wills are changeable and revocable. Patients may withdraw or make changes to Advance Directives, including Living Wills at any time.

Among the many resources available, patients and families may consider the following resources for information and protocols specific to individual states for preparing Advance Directives:

The American Bar Association

740 15th Street, N.W.
Washington, DC 20005
800-285-2221

Or

321 North Clark Street
Chicago, IL 60654
312-988-5000
http://www.americanbar.org

U.S. Living Will Registry

23 Westfield Ave., P.O. Box 2789
Westfield, NJ 07091-2789
1-800-548-9455
http://www.uslivingwillregistry.com

Two by Two

Consider Mark 6:7. *"And he called unto him the twelve, and began to send them forth by two and two; and gave them power over unclean spirits;"* Matthew 21:1 states *"And when they drew nigh unto Jerusalem, and were come to Bethphage, unto the mount of Olives, then sent Jesus two disciples."* In 1 Samuel 15:22, Samuel asked the question, *"...Hath the LORD as great delight in burnt offerings and sacrifices, as in obeying the voice of the LORD? Behold, to obey is better than sacrifice, and to hearken than the fat of rams."* Jesus determined to send His disciples out two by two. It is His lead that we obey and follow. Consider the apostles, Peter and John, in Acts 3:1-4.

> *Now Peter and John went up together into the temple at the hour of prayer, being the ninth hour. And a certain man lame from his mother's womb was carried, whom they laid daily at the gate of the temple which is called Beautiful, to ask alms of them that entered into the temple; Who seeing Peter and John about to go into the temple asked an alms. And Peter, fastening his eyes upon him with John, said, Look on us."* [emphasis added]

When you have another minister with you, you are ensuring that you witness and share the same experience. In this way, you are able to watch and cover each other in prayer.

Traveling with another minister also helps to alleviate misunderstandings and liabilities. The Apostle Paul, in Romans 10:2 said of a people whom God loves most affectionately, *"For I bear them record that they have a zeal of God, but not according to knowledge."*

Although you may be enthusiastic and willing to go alone, always take another minister with you. It is for your protection. It is wisdom. It is God's way. Proverbs 4:7 teaches, *"Wisdom is the principal thing; therefore get wisdom: and with all thy getting get understanding."*

Part Five

Counsel and Comfort

"Who comforteth us in all our tribulation, that we may be able to comfort them which are in any trouble, by the comfort wherewith we ourselves are comforted of God."

11 Corinthians 1:4

Helping Patients and Families Make Tough Decisions

Chronic or sudden serious illness can force individuals and families to face difficult life decisions and grapple with quality of life issues in determining what, if any, concessions have to be made in prolonging or sustaining life. You may meet with a family that believes their loved one requires mechanical ventilation in order to stay alive. Sometimes patients become exhausted and worn out from aggressive treatments and medication side effects and, together with their families, are considering hospice care.

Another major decision families face when a member is suffering chronic illness is whether to place their family member in a facility for long-term care or keep their loved one at home. Family members may express the desire to care for loved ones at home, yet feel overwhelmed by work schedules, child rearing or space limitations.

You may witness tensions mount as families wrestle with the implications of each. Often, at the root of indecision are feelings of powerlessness, fear, fatigue, guilt, and sometimes shame. You may be asked to render an opinion about what a patient or family should do. "What," you may ask, "should I say?"

As a minister of the gospel, you are charged with believing the whole gospel of Jesus Christ. That is to believe upon Jesus' desire and promises of healing as well as His sovereign allowances for greater glory and ministry to arise out of the ashes of death and despair. Jesus, who could have prevented his own death as illustrated in Matthew 26:53 and Hebrews 12:2, decided to die so that others might live. Jesus' death ushered in the fulfillment of God's plan for the provision of life here and in eternity for humankind. Remember, God's plan is always for life beyond the immediate circumstance.

While patients and families may ask for your opinion when facing major healthcare decisions, consider a word of caution to refrain from yielding your opinion and, instead, engage the patient and family in discussions (several if needed) about their individual feelings. Find a convenient time and quiet place (aside from the patient's room) to pray and converse with family members. Assure confidentiality as you invite individual family members to share their feelings.

If the patient is able to converse with you, hold a private conversation with the patient as well. Assure the patient of confidentiality and listen with compassion.

There may be times when, apart from family members, a patient confides in you the desire to depart from this life. Sometimes, patients will talk about being tired and wanting to "go home." Patients will often try to will themselves to resist death to appease family members who are not ready to let the patient go. Suffering is a highly subjective and individual experience. The Holy Spirit is, in reality, the only One who genuinely understands what a suffering individual experiences. Often, when a patient dies, families are left wondering if their prayers for healing were ever heard. Consider the omniscience of the Holy Spirit who allows for divine intercession for patients as well as family members. Consider Romans 8:26-27.

> *Likewise the Spirit also helpeth our infirmities: for we know not what we should pray for as we ought: but the Spirit itself maketh intercession for us with groanings which cannot be uttered. And he that searcheth the hearts knoweth what is the mind of the Spirit, because he maketh intercession for the saints according to the will of God.*

Sometimes, the Holy Spirit chooses to answer the silent prayer of the patient for relief from earthly pain through eternal fellowship with Jesus.

As a member of the clergy, you serve as a compassionate guide in assisting families in making difficult decisions. In providing counseling, you allow patients and their families to explore and share their concerns. Pray with and for patients and their families that the peace of God will guide their hearts. Remember, it is most beneficial for patients and their families to arrive at their own conclusions. For only then can every conscience rest, including yours.

Your consistent prayers, support and compassion minister the love of God that patients and families need. Even when feeling tempted or pressured to tell patients or their families what you think should be done, remember the wise words of the Apostle Paul. *"All things are lawful for me, but all things are not expedient. All things are lawful for me, but all things edify not"* (*1 Corinthians 10:23*).

When Death Seems Imminent

When death seems imminent, family members may become discouraged and ask you what to do. A patient may begin to share with you what her wishes are upon passing away. Continue to pray with the patient and family for healing and believe God. However, be careful to listen with understanding and patience.

Prayerfully avoid judging either the patient or her family when conversations about death arise. Remember that faith for healing remains, even in the midst of preparing for death. Sometimes, a patient has already decided that she wants to be with Jesus. Patients who are near death often speak and dream of their experience as well. It is quite usual to hear patients mention loved ones who have passed away. Patients may even report seeing departed loved ones or having spiritual experiences involving angels and even the Lord, Jesus.

In your capacity as a minister, be careful to allow patients to share and confide in you about their experiences, if desired. You may have opportunities to minister the assurance of salvation in the midst of patient fears and uncertainties. Your understanding, non-judgmental approach and *active* listening will quell anxieties associated with reconciling imminent departure from this life. As well, patients who share their experiences with you are demonstrating trust in your ability to be sensitive and affirming. Remember, patients who are gravely ill and approaching death will rarely, if at all, waste words.

You may consider speaking with the family about practical considerations relating to the passing of their loved one as you or the family perceives death approaching. However, it is usually best to allow the family to initiate any discussion about any possibility of the patient passing away. If it appears that the family is unprepared for a patient's imminent passing, and you have developed a rapport with the family that would allow you to be a part of such a discussion, consider the following.

If a patient's family members *voluntarily* discuss with you the prognosis or concerns of the patient's physician, sympathetically engage family members in a conversation about their feelings. In so doing, ask supportive questions that guide family members through the thought process of decision-making. Guide the conversation to focus the patient's wishes.

At times, you may find that patients are more resolute with possible outcomes than are family members. Patients may attempt to discuss their feeling with family members and make final preparations. Often, friends or family members experience awkwardness when patients attempt to say good-bye or give instructions. You may notice family members or friends changing the subject or being dismissive of patients' attempts toward sober conversations about death. Be careful to refrain from judging anyone, either inwardly or by outward expression.

Sometimes, individuals are unprepared to accept the thought of life without their loved one. Moreover, family members or friends may equate resistance to death to a demonstration of faith for healing, so that, for them, any acceptance of impending death denies the power of faith.

Family members should be advised of what physical signs to look for and who should be called if a patient dies. Some of the signs can include consistent extremely low blood pressure, the gradual cessation of speech, the cessation of food or fluid intake, sharp decreases in bodily functions (system shutdown) and continual sleeping. End of life indicators can also include 'noisy breathing.' Noisy breathing is a term medical professionals use to describe a gargling sound emanating from a patient's throat area as air passes through mucus in a patient's throat when breathing. Whether a patient dies at home or in a hospital facility, this can be an extremely distressing time for family members.

Organ and Tissue Donation

Organ donation is a subject likely to arise in two situations: one, when one person's life can be saved or extended by the transplant of healthy organs, tissue or blood from another living person or two, where medical personnel believe that the impending death of one patient can result in the prolonging of life for another.[1] If a patient becomes a candidate for organ, tissue or blood transplants, family members or other loved ones may test for positive matches to see if the donation can be made safely. Absent a viable match from family or friends, a patient may be placed on the National Transplant Waiting List. Healthcare personnel and representatives from organ donation organizations assist the patient and the patient's family in navigating the process of preparing for a transplant, which includes ongoing care, insurance and financial considerations.

In the case of impending death resulting from sudden or grave incapacity of an otherwise healthy individual, healthcare personnel may approach family members about organ and tissue donation. Representatives of Organ Procurement Organizations (OPO) are usually on call at hospitals to speak with families when recommended. Organ procurement

---

[1] Committee, OPTN/UNOS Patient Affairs. "Talking About Transplantation: What Every Patient Needs to Know." United Network for Organ Sharing, 2011.

organizations staff personnel who work in conjunction with patients, patients' families and medical personnel to facilitate the process of transplantation of donated organs.

A patient's family may encounter a representative from an OPO if a physician certifies that a patient's brain activity has irreversibly ceased. Medical personnel define the cessation of brain activity as the end of life although a patient may be kept alive artificially. If this occurs, a patient's organs and tissues may remain functional for a time. Some organ and tissue transplants can take place immediately upon a patient's expiration. However, to be successful, there are other transplants, like the heart, which requires that life remains in the donating patient's body when it is removed.

Families are often faced with difficult decisions about quality of life and organ donations when sudden incapacity occurs. It can be problematic for family members to ascertain what their loved one would decide. Unless otherwise indicated on one's driver's license or state registry, organ and tissue donation wishes remain with the patient and the patient's family. Individuals and families may benefit from having this discussion in advance of any need for immediate decision-making.

Note: Some patients and/or families decline to participate in organ and tissue donations of any sort, including blood transfusions, because of religious beliefs. Refrain from judging or expressing opposing opinions to patients' or families' convictions. Trust God to heal by his grace and remain supportive at all times.

There are many resources available for individuals and families seeking more information about organ and tissue donation and transplantation. Among them are the following.

The U.S. Department of Health and Human Services

200 Independence Avenue, S.W.
Washington, D.C. 20201
Toll Free: 1-877-696-6775
http://www.organdonor.gov

Partnering With Your Transplant Team: A Patient's Guide to Transplantation

A booklet prepared by the United Network for Organ Sharing (UNOS http://optn.transplant.hrsa.gov/ContentDocuments/ PartneringWithTransplantTeam_508v.pdf

National Living Donor Assistance Center (NLDAC)

2461 S. Clark Street, Suite 640
Arlington, VA 22202
Phone: 703.414.1600
Toll Free: 888.870.5002
http://livingdonorassistance.org/

The National Minority Organ and Tissue Transplant Education Program

903 D Street, 2nd Floor
Washington, DC 20002-6127
240 280 9410
http://www.mottep.org/

Understanding Hospice Care

Hospice is a form of palliative care for patients who have been diagnosed as having a terminal illness and who have declined to establish or continue aggressive treatments. Palliative Care is care with the objective of keeping the patient comfortable and out of pain as much as possible. Aggressive treatments include surgeries, transplants, experimental drug treatments, participation in research trials or various therapies like dialysis, radiation and chemotherapy.

To be considered for hospice care, a patient's physician certifies that the patient has a life expectancy of six months or less. Hospice care transitions patients from aggressive life extending treatment to efforts to maintain quality of life, which usually consist of pain control and maintaining the patient's physical comfort.

Doctors and nurses devise individualized hospice care plans for each patient by taking into account the patient's medical history and requests for the future. The development of the patient's care plan may involve input from the patient's family in decision-making, especially when considering whether the patient is served at home or moved to a hospice care facility.

For patients transferring to hospice care it is important that patients and families understand the decision to discontinue life-prolonging therapies as hospice providers place exclusive emphasis on keeping patients comfortable.

One of the first requests of patients by healthcare personnel when discussing hospice care is to sign a DNR. The reason patients in hospice care are requested to sign a DNR is that the premise of hospice precludes any interference with the natural course of life and death.

Patients in hospice care may receive oral and/or intravenous pain medication. However, other forms of intravenous therapies including fluids to prevent dehydration or liquid feeding are usually exempt from the care plan.

When visiting patients in hospice care you may encounter distress on the part of family members concerned about patient care in regard to eating and drinking. One reason for this is that medical personnel define hospice as an *end of life* plan of care that would be impeded by forcing liquids or food into the body. Patients' family members may request liquids or nutrition to be given intravenously, but should know that patient discomfort, including swelling of the stomach, arms and legs can sometimes occur with forced feeding.

Of additional concern for patients suffering through particular diseases is difficulty swallowing. In noting patient difficulty with swallowing, especially liquids, medical personnel may caution family members of the necessity to carefully avoid aspiration. Aspiration is the process of liquid or food particles entering the bronchi and lungs in the effort to breathe. Aspiration can be an extremely painful and distressing experience for patients, not to mention life threatening.

Again, conventional thinking in hospice care suggests that the objective is to keep patients comfortable and out of pain as much as possible while allowing life in the body to take its natural course. As such, patients who are nearing the end of life may have fewer needs for the consumption of food and liquids. Additionally, the cessation of medical treatments acts as a relief from the harrowing experiences patients sometimes have from strong medications and aggressive therapies.

In hospice settings it is normal to observe a decline in patient health over time. As patients begin to decline, families may begin to notice patient weight loss and loss of appetite along with decreasing ability to concentrate for long periods. Eventually, the patient may begin to speak and converse less. Patients may also begin to sleep more. Further decline is often noted with a drop in a patient's blood pressure to undetectable levels and noisy breathing.

Patients or families who are interested in locating hospice facilities or resources may consider the following organizations:

Hospice Foundation of America

1710 Rhode Island Ave, NW
Suite 400
Washington, DC 20036
(800) 854-3402 or (202) 457-5811
http://www.hospicefoundation.org

National Hospice and Palliative Care Organization

1731 King Street, Suite 100
Alexandria, Virginia 22314
(800) 658 -8898 or 703/837-1500
http://www.nhpco.org

What to Do if a Patient Dies

If a patient dies at a healthcare facility, the patient's physician will certify the death and contact the family via telephone unless the family is already present. Family members may be asked to collect the patient's effects and provide the name of the funeral director to whom their loved one will be released. Depending on the prior health of the patient family members may be asked to donate one or more of the patient's organs, for example. Family members should take the time needed to make informed decisions should the request arise.

If a patient expires at home, family members should immediately contact the patient's physician and then Emergency Medical Services (EMS) or the police. If the patient is in hospice care at home, family members should immediately call the hospice coordinator, who will call the patient's physician and the police. Families of hospice patients at home would have been provided a twenty-four hour emergency telephone number for hospice care. When EMS or the police arrive at the home the family will need to provide information as to whom the patient's body will be entrusted. Family members should call a funeral director to arrange for pick-up of their loved one.

Aftercare for the Family

When a loved one dies, family members grieve individually and corporately. Some people may grieve longer than others may. It is important to note that grieving individuals need to mourn, that is to find ways to safely express their grief. Some people immediately return to work or school. For other individuals, keeping busy with hobbies or social activities is a way of mourning. One person may withdraw from outside activities altogether for a while. These are all forms of mourning. Mourning is the manner in which a person expresses grief. Mourning is the outlet for expressing grief.

Internalized, unexpressed grief can be unhealthy emotionally, psychologically and physically. Understanding the difference between grief and mourning is important as this knowledge enables you to offer compassionate guidance to grieving families and individuals.

One phrase grieving families hear often is, *"If there is anything I can do, please let me know."* Well-meaning friends, associates, colleagues and even ministers leave grieving family members with this trite suggestion unaware that the grief stricken are often overwhelmed and ill-prepared to make the effort needed to garner assistance. Grief can be so debilitating that individuals can find themselves devoid of the mental or emotional strength to reach out to others for support. Often, rather than think of whom to call for what, emotionally depleted, grieving family members attempt to handle affairs alone.

For one, the grieving family may be quite aware that friends and other loved ones have their own family and work responsibilities to return to after the formalities of planning and completing memorial services have concluded. Secondly, grieving families may feel that their requests for assistance may be a bother to others, including busy pastors and ministers. As well, grieving individuals may want the fellowship of a supportive friend or minister just for conversation or company and feel unable to make the request. Sometimes grieving family members need support and are unsure of how to express their needs.

As a minister, your efforts toward reaching out to the family gently and consistently over time will prove an invaluable support. Without placing the responsibility upon the family to make a need known to you, find time to reach out and stay close. Know in advance that there *is* something you can do and that is to be present and in the moment. Take the initiative to, *"Rejoice with them that do rejoice, and weep with them that weep" (Romans 12:15).* You are well equipped to minister the enabling grace of God to provide help in times of need (Hebrews 4:16).

Keep in mind that your compassionate support refrains from judgment about the length of the grieving process or the manner of mourning one chooses. Always remember, your objectives as a minister are to exercise wisdom and lean to the guidance of the Holy Spirit that you may walk in the anointing to "...bind up the brokenhearted" with grace (Isaiah 61:1b).

Conclusion

"Let us hear the conclusion of the whole matter: Fear God, and keep his commandments: for this is the whole duty of man."

Ecclesiastes 12:13

"Jesus said unto him, Thou shalt love the Lord thy God with all thy heart, and with all thy soul, and with all thy mind. This is the first and great commandment. And the second is like unto it, Thou shalt love thy neighbour as thyself. On these two commandments hang all the law and the prophets."

Matthew 22:37-40

Pleasing the Audience of One

"...and thy Father, which seeth in secret, shall reward thee openly."

Visiting the sick is one of the most benevolent and dutiful acts you will carry out as a minister. The manner in which you undertake your responsibility will determine how God and those you visit receive your gift. It is important to evaluate your objective in embarking upon the charge to visit the sick. Compassion, as a motivating force, seeks simply to relieve the suffering of others.

Remember how Jesus was moved with compassion when He observed people suffering? *"And Jesus went forth, and saw a great multitude, and was moved with compassion toward them, and he healed their sick"* *(Matthew 14:14).* Compassion is birthed out of empathy - that is the experience of relating to others' pain and suffering. When your purpose for visiting the sick is founded in an authentic desire to represent the Balm in Gilead, healing results - many times observably.

One might suggest that visiting the sick is a thankless ministry. However, in considering the meaning of thankless, regard it as it a blessing. A thankless action is an action that is denied acknowledgement, appreciation, reward or reciprocity - by man, that is. When you, for example, visit a patient who is sleeping and pray quietly in the doorway before leaving, the patient is unaware of your visit, but Jesus is. Jesus *is* the *Audience of One.*

Acknowledgement, appreciation, reward and reciprocity are befitting anticipations when the Father is the object of those hopes. Any ambition or craving, however subtle, for public recognition yields, at best, a temporal nodding at the price of eternal reward. *"But lay up for yourselves treasures in heaven, where neither moth nor rust doth corrupt, and where thieves do not break through nor steal" (Matthew 6:20).*

How can you tell if the audience you seek to please is made up of the *Audience of One* or more than one, including self? How do you know if you are seeking the applause of man? Confidence in Jesus as the *Audience of One* brings satisfaction that is complete. However, inner needs for affirmation and applause can often impel one to self-promotion.

For instance, one may consciously or unconsciously plan or hope to visit when one is sure others are present to observe, praise and spread the word. Or, one may talk piously about making particular visits and the personal sacrifices involved or the miracles performed at one's hands. Individuals seeking an audience of many may self-importantly disregard hospital protocols or break patient or family confidences under the guise of heeding the Spirit's call or galvanizing prayer partners and support. Pride is at the route of every conscious and unconscious effort to bypass the *Audience of One* for the audience of many.

The working of miracles at the apostles' hands resulted from the apostles' commitment to Jesus as the *Audience of One*. Although the apostles were the vessels through whom the power of the Holy Spirit flowed, of notable mention is the fact that the apostles ensured that the healings resulted in praises to God alone. Consider Acts 3:1-13a.

> *Now Peter and John went up together into the temple at the hour of prayer, being the ninth hour. And a certain man lame from his mother's womb was carried, whom they laid daily at the gate of the temple which is called Beautiful, to ask alms of them that entered into the temple; Who seeing Peter and John about to go into the temple asked an alms. And Peter, fastening his eyes upon him with John, said, Look on us. And he gave heed unto them, expecting to receive something of them. Then Peter said, Silver and gold have I none; but such as I have give I thee: In the name of Jesus Christ of Nazareth rise up and walk. And he took him by the right hand, and lifted him up: and immediately his feet and ankle bones received strength. And he leaping up*

stood, and walked, and entered with them into the temple, walking, and leaping, and praising God. And all the people saw him walking and praising God. And they knew that it was he which sat for alms at the Beautiful gate of the temple: and they were filled with wonder and amazement at that which had happened unto him. And as the lame man which was healed held Peter and John, all the people ran together unto them in the porch that is called Solomon's, greatly wondering. And when Peter saw it, he answered unto the people, **Ye men of Israel, why marvel ye at this? or why look ye so earnestly on us, as though by our own power or holiness we had made this man to walk? The God of Abraham, and of Isaac, and of Jacob, the God of our fathers, hath glorified his Son Jesus;** [emphasis added]

While at times the recipients of God's healing demonstrated honor and appreciation to the Lord's servants as in Acts 28:10, the apostles were careful to forbid themselves or others to mistake the human for the Divine. *"And as Peter was coming in, Cornelius met him and fell down at his feet, and worshipped him. But Peter took him up, saying, Stand up; I myself also am a man"* (Acts 10:25-26).

The more singularly focused you become in pleasing the *Audience of One*, the more miracles will flow. As demonstrated by Jesus, love ought to be the impetus or motivation for ministering healing. The Apostle Paul reiterates this by his declaration in 1 Corinthians 13: 1-3 (NLT).

If I could speak all the languages of earth and of angels, but didn't love others, I would only be a noisy gong or a clanging cymbal. If I had the gift of prophecy, and if I understood all of God's secret plans and possessed all knowledge, and if I had such faith that I could move mountains, but didn't love others, I would be nothing. If I gave everything I have [including my time] *to the poor* [including the poor in health] *and even sacrificed my body, I could boast about it, but if I didn't love others, I would have gained nothing.*

Allow the Holy Spirit to minister through you readily and without encumbrances rooted in fear, sin-consciousness, hidden motives, self-sufficiency or pride. Remember that Jesus heals by His grace and the *Audience of One* is the only audience that matters. Diligence in seeking the Lord as your One and true audience births the insight and truthfulness required for authenticity in ministry.

Understanding the ministry of the Holy Spirit and His grace will help you to focus on Jesus' sacrifice and Jesus' faith rather than on your faith or your works. *"For by grace are [we] saved through faith; and that not of [ourselves]: it is the gift of God: Not of works, lest any man should boast" (Ephesians 2:8-9).* Healing, like salvation, is the result of God's grace. Remember Romans 8:1-4.

There is therefore now no condemnation to them which are in Christ Jesus, who walk not after the flesh, but after the Spirit. For the law of the Spirit of life in Christ Jesus hath made me free from the law of sin and death. For what the law could not do, in that it was weak through the flesh, God sending his own Son in the likeness of sinful flesh, and for sin, condemned sin [disallowing sickness to reign] *in the flesh: That the righteousness of the law might be fulfilled in us, who walk not after the flesh, but after the Spirit.*

When tempted to doubt the significance of your sacrifice, especially when faced with personal trials and tribulations, rehearse the words of Jesus, *"... Inasmuch as ye have done it unto one of the least of these my brethren, ye have done it unto me"* (Matthew 25:40). Know that the Father takes every effort on your part to be a conduit through which He can minister His grace to the broken and the suffering very seriously.

Hospitals are filled with the infirmed of body, mind and spirit. Hospitals are fields white unto harvest and you are a laborer that the Father longs to use. Your ministry is both needed and appreciated by the One who is well able to affirm you. Remember, *"But without faith it is impossible to please him: for he that cometh to God must believe that he is, and that he is a rewarder of them that diligently seek him"* (Hebrews 11:6).

To maintain a comforting, faithful, lasting and authentic presence in the lives of patients suffering illness is a worthy, selfless and spiritual undertaking from which the fearful, law-conscious, or those seeking recognition, including the prideful, pretentious, chronically busy, or faint of heart eventually shy away. But, be not weary in well doing, for in due season you *will* reap. God's grace will keep you from fainting (Galatians 6:9).

"And whatsoever ye do, do it heartily, as to the Lord, and not unto men; Knowing that of the Lord ye shall receive the reward of the inheritance: for ye serve [the Audience of One, who is] *the Lord Christ"* (Colossians 3:23-24).

Thank you for purchasing the
Hospital Visitation Guide for Ministers.

Surely, Jesus appreciates your interest in learning more about the comfort and joy your presence brings to those suffering illness.

The **Hospital Visitation Guide for Ministers** is part of a leadership-training curriculum designed to prepare leaders in various aspects of service to the Body of Christ and community.

For further information about workshops and training sessions for you or your leaders, please contact us at **Leaders@HospitalVisitations.com.**

Additional copies of this book may be obtained from your local or online bookstore or at our web-site, **www.HospitalVisitations.com.**

Resources

Advance Directives

The American Bar Association
740 15th Street, N.W.
Washington, DC 20005
800-285-2221

Or

321 North Clark Street
Chicago, IL 60654
312-988-5000
http://www.americanbar.org

U.S. Living Will Registry
523 Westfield Ave., P.O. Box 2789
Westfield, NJ 07091-2789
1-800-548-9455
http://www.uslivingwillregistry.com

Care Giving

Administration on Aging
Washington, DC 20201
Office of the Assistant Secretary for Aging:
(202) 401-4634
Public Inquiries: (202) 619-0724
http://www.aoa.gov/AoARoot/index.aspx

Care Giving Help
3003 W. Touhy Avenue
Chicago, IL 60645
Telephone 773.508.1000
Fax 773.508.1070
http://www.caregivinghelp.org/contact

United States Department of Veterans Affairs Caregiver Support
810 Vermont Avenue, NW
Washington, DC 20420
1-800-827-1000 / TDD 1-800-829-4833
http://www.caregiver.va.gov

Health and Life Insurance Information and Referrals

Centers for Medicare & Medicaid Services
7500 Security Boulevard
Baltimore MD 21244-1850
1800-633-2273
http://www.medicare.gov

U.S. Department of Veterans Affairs
810 Vermont Avenue, NW
Washington, DC 20420
1-800-827-1000

Veterans' Life Insurance
Service members and/or Veterans Group Life Insurance Program
1-800-419-1473

All other VA Life Insurance Programs
1-800-669-8477
http://www.va.gov

Hospice Information and Services

Hospice Foundation of America
1710 Rhode Island Ave, NW
Suite 400
Washington, DC 20036
(800) 854-3402 or (202) 457-5811
http://www.hospicefoundation.org.

National Hospice and Palliative Care Organization
1731 King Street, Suite 100
Alexandria, Virginia 22314
(800) 658 -8898 or 703/837-1500
http://www.nhpco.org

Organ Donation and Transplant Services

The U.S. Department of Health and Human Services
200 Independence Avenue, S.W.
Washington, D.C. 20201
Toll Free: 1-877-696-6775
http://www.organdonor.gov

Partnering With Your Transplant Team:
A Patient's Guide to Transplantation
A booklet prepared by the United Network for Organ Sharing (UNOS
http://optn.transplant.hrsa.gov/ContentDocum
ents/PartneringWithTransplantTeam_508v.pdf

National Living Donor Assistance Center
2461 S. Clark Street, Suite 640
Arlington, VA 22202
Phone: 703.414.1600 / Toll Free: 888.870.5002
http://livingdonorassistance.org

The National Minority Organ and Tissue
Transplant Education Program
903 D Street- 2nd Floor
Washington, DC 20002-6127
240 280 9410
http://www.mottep.org

National Council on Aging: National Center
for Benefits Outreach & Enrollment
1901 L Street, NW - 4th Floor
Washington, D.C. 20036
202.479.1200
http://www.benefitscheckup.org/

Social Security Administration

Social Security Administration
Office of Public Inquiries
Windsor Park Building
6401 Security Blvd.
Baltimore, MD 21235
1-800-772-1213 TTY 1-800-325-0778
http://www.ssa.gov

Index

Acknowledgement, Seeking............................152

Administration on Aging 164

Advance Directives..........................109, 163

    and Quality of Life 114

    Choosing..........................116

    Do Not Resuscitate (DNR) 112, 139

    Durable Power of Attorney..........................112

    Healthcare Proxy..........................111

    Living Will 110, 163

    Power of Attorney for Healthcare..........................110

    Resources 119, 163

After Praying for a Patient 95

Aftercare for the Family..........................144

American Bar Association..........................119, 163

Anointing With Oil.......................... 19

Audience of One..........................151

Avoiding the Spread of Infection 33

Bacteria 34

Balm in Gilead..........................152

Baptism

    At Bedside..........................76

    Avoiding Liability 80

    Full Immersion..........................79

    Hospital Personnel..........................78

    Illustration 81

    Permission 79

    Saftety..........................79

    Significance of 77

Before Entering a Patient's Room 59
Caregiver Support 164
Centers for Medicare & Medicaid Services 107, 165
Clergy Identification 27
Compassion 151
    and Healing 17
Concern About Treatment 46
Conclusion 149
Confidence in self 153
Contagions 36
Contagious Diseases 43
Counsel and Comfort 123
Debates 57
Decorum
    Conversation 53
    Appeaarance 54
    Discussions and Debates 57
    Giving Advice 57
    Organization 56
    Speech 55
    Mobile Phones 56
    Proper 53
Defibrillation 113
Diet Restricttions 48
Displays of Emotion 22
DNR Order 113
Entering a Patient's Room 64
Faith, Mustard Seed 17
Flowers 47
Food 47

Fungi 34
General Protocols...25
Germs...33
   and Hospital Room Curtains....................................38
   Bacteria..34
   Fungi..34
   Parasites 35
   Viruses...34
Gloves...42
Grief and Mourning....................................144
Hand Hygiene...32, 40
Hand Sanitizer..42
   and Gloves 42
Hand Washing Procedure 40
Health Insurance Portability and
   Accountability Act (HIPAA) 45
Healthcare Personnel..................................61
Healthcare-Associated Infections 36
Helping Families
   Through Grief 144
Helping Patients and Families
   Make Tough Decisions...............................125
   When Death Seems Imminent 129
Holy Communion 86
   Prayer for 87
   Sample..87
Hospice Care
   and Aggressive Therapy...........................138
   and DNR..139
   and Food and Drink.................................140

End of Life..140

Resources 142, 166

Understanding..................................138

Hospice Foundation of America....................... 142, 166

Hospital Visiting Hours.............................. 29

If You are Sick 23

Infection, Concerns About 43

Insurance, Health and Life 105, 165

Veterans.................................108, 165

Introduction 3

Leading a Person to Christ 70

Leaving a Patient's Room.............................96

Living Wills................................117, 163

Love 5

Methicillin-resistant Staphylcoccus aureus
(MRSA)... 36

Mobile Phones 56

National Council on Aging: National Center for
Benefits Outreach & Enrollment.................... 107, 168

National Hospice and Palliative Care
Organization.....................................142, 166

National Living Donor Assistance Center......... 137, 167

National Minority Organ and Tissue Transplant
Education Program 137, 168

Nervousness, While Visiting 22

Non Per Os.. 48

Obtaining Visitors' Passes 29

Organ and Tissue Donation 133

Resources 136, 167

Palliative Care..138

Parasites 35
Parking 28
Patient
    Comfort 69
    Information 27
    Privacy 45
    Salvation 70
Patients
    Dying 93
    Isolation 62
    Reverse Isolation 64
    Sedated, Unconscious or Comatose 92
    Sleeping 91
Patients' Belongings 38, 65
Personal Protective Equipment (PPE) 44
Practical Insights 103
Prayer
    A Lifestyle of 15
    For Healing 85
    Importance of 15
Preface 1
Pregnancy
    and infections 39, 63
Preparation 11
    Sample Prayer of 14
Preparing to Pray for a Patient 68
Quality of Life 114
    and CPR 115

Resources
    Advance Directives 119, 163
    Care Giving....................................164
    Department of Veterans Affairs.............. 107, 165
    Hospice Information and Services............. 142, 166
    Life and Health Insurance................. 107, 165
    Medicare and Medicaid................... 107, 165
    Organ Donation and Transplant Services...... 136, 167
Scriptures
    Baptism 83
    Healing...7
    Holy Communion..............................89
    Salvation.......................................72
Sharing Scripture................................. 67
Social Security Administration 168
Tetracyclines.................................... 39
Thank you...................................... 161
The Holy Spirit as Healer....................... 157
The National Minority Organ and Tissue Transplant
    Education Program 168
U.S. Department of Health and
    Human Services 136, 167
U.S. Department of Veterans Affairs............107, 164
U.S. Living Will Registry....................120, 163
Unclean Hands 42
Universal Precautions 32
Viruses... 34

Visiting
 a Patient 51
 Babies 97
 the Chronically Ill 101
 the Elderly..98
 the Mentally Ill 99
 Two by Two...120
 While Pregnant 39, 63
 With Gifts 47
 With Wisdom...120
Visiting Babies..97
Visits Begin At Home 13
Web-site
 HospitalVisitations.com...........................161
What to Do
 After a Visit..96
 If a Patient Dies...143
When To Visit 23, 29
When Hospital Personnel Are Present........61
Wisdom..25, 53, 82

Notes

Notes

Notes

2744003R00105

Made in the USA
San Bernardino, CA
31 May 2013